The Bible of Medicinal Plants

Save Thousands with the Complete Beginners Guide On: Planting, Growing, and Harvesting Plants and Herbs to Use in Your Daily Life

J.P.RAE

Copyright 2022 - All rights reserved.

The content contained within this book may not be reproduced, duplicated, or transmitted without direct written permission from the author or the publisher.

Under no circumstances will any blame or legal responsibility be held against the publisher, or author, for any damages, reparation, or monetary loss due to the information contained within this book, either directly or indirectly.

Legal Notice:

This book is copyright protected. It is only for personal use. You cannot amend, distribute, sell, use, quote, or paraphrase any part, or the content within this book, without the consent of the author or publisher.

Disclaimer Notice:

Please note the information contained within this document is for educational and entertainment purposes only. All effort has been executed to present accurate, up-to-date, reliable, complete information. No warranties of any kind are declared or implied. Readers acknowledge that the author is not engaged in rendering legal, financial, medical, or professional advice. The content within this book has been derived from various sources. Please consult a licensed professional before attempting any techniques outlined in this book.

By reading this document, the reader agrees that under no circumstances is the author responsible for any direct or indirect losses incurred as a result of the use of the information contained within this document, including, but not limited to, errors, omissions, or inaccuracies

"There are no incurable diseases, only the lack of will. There are no worthless herbs, only the lack of knowledge."

– Avicenna

A SPECIAL GIFT TO OUR READERS

Herewith your purchase of this book we have included a gift to help you get prepared for the future. Herbal Medicine 101 will not only let you discover more about herbal remedies but let you get involved in the community. This is the key to opening the door for starting your journey.

Scan the QR code below and let us know what email is best to deliver it to.

Table of Contents

Introduction 1
Chapter 1: Gardening 101 4
    A Garden Requires Dedication and Consistency 5
    Starting a Backyard Garden 7
    Starting with Potting 11
    Tips to Start 11
    Best Potting Mix to Start Sowing Seeds 14
    How to Sow Seeds 14
    Reading the Package of Seeds 15
    Step-by-Step Guide on How to Start 15
    Types of Herb Gardens 18
    Bee Garden 18
    Medieval Garden 18
    Shakespeare Garden 18
    Indoor Herb Garden 19
    Gray and Silver Garden 19
    Fragrance Garden 19
    Permaculture 19

History of Permaculture 20

Rudolf Steiner 21

Understanding Permaculture and Biodynamic Farming 21

Greenhouses 22

How to Start a Greenhouse 23

Water and Drainage Outdoor Gardens 24

Organic Gardening 25

Chapter 2: The Perfect Space 28

Soil 28

Soil pH 31

How to Optimize Your Soil Naturally 32

Composting 33

Exposure 34

Wind Exposure 35

Sun Exposure 35

The Best Exposure for a Garden 36

The Best Geographical Location to Grow Herbs 37

Chapter 3: Planting 39

The Importance of Buying Organic Seeds 39

Planting Seeds 41

Difficulties You May Encounter When Planting Seeds 44

Planting from Division and What Is It? 45

Planting from Cuttings and What Is It? 46

Potting 47

Repotting 48

Why Should Certain Herbs Not Be Planted Together?
....51

How to Start a Small Herbal Permaculture Garden .52

Chapter 4: Maintaining 55

The Importance of Maintaining Your Herb Garden 55

Watering Your Herbs..56

Trimming Your Herbs 57

Pruning Your Herbs...58

Staking Your Herbs..59

Pest Control 61

Common Diseases of an Herb Garden....................62

Natural Fertilizers for Herbs 64

DIY..66

Create the Best Compost 67

Why You Need to Prepare your Herbs for Winter and How to Do It...68

Low-Maintenance Herbs 69

High-Maintenance Herbs..71

Chapter 5: Harvesting 73

Harvesting Herbs 101 73

Why Is It Important to Harvest Herbs at the Right Time 75

Tips to Harvest Herbs 76

Most Common Herb Gardening Mistakes 77

When Should You Harvest? 79

What Time is Best to Harvest Herbs 79

When to Harvest Leaves 80

When to Harvest Flowers 81

When to Harvest Roots 82

Harvesting Herbs According to the Moon Cycle 82

Chapter 6: Medicinal Herbs to Grow 84

What Are Medicinal Herbs? 85

History of Medicinal Herbs 86

Native American 86

Chinese 89

Ayurveda 91

10 Easy to Grow Herbs and Their Properties 92

Basil 92

Mint 94

Chives 95

Parsley 96

Rosemary 97

Oregano 98

Thyme 99

Dill 99

Sage 100

Coriander 101
10 Not-as-Easy Herbs to Grow and Their Properties
.... 102
Lavender 103
Dandelion 104
Yarrow 105
Stinging Nettle 106
Calendula 107
Chamomile 107
Fennel 108
Bay 109
Stevia 110
Lemongrass 110
Perennial Herbs 112
Annual Herbs 112

Chapter 7: Preparations 114
Drying Herbs 114
Rack Drying 115
Hanging Drying 115
Oven Drying 116
Microwave Drying 117
How to Store Dried Herbs 117
How to Store Fresh Herbs 118
Infusions with Fresh Herbs 120

Herbal Tea 121

Herb Powder 122

Tinctures 123

Oil Extract 125

Infusing Herbs in Honey 126

Infusing Herbs in Vinegar 127

Chapter 8: Cooking 129

Benefits of Using Herbs Every Day 129

Ways to Use Herbs in Your Kitchen Daily 131

Recipes with Herbs 132

Spiced Chicken and Cilantro Lime Butter 133

Herbed Feta Dip 134

Rosemary Focaccia 134

Herb Butter 136

Cheddar and Chive Mashed Potatoes 136

Green Beans with Fresh Herbs 137

Cilantro Lime Shrimp 138

Dill Cheesy Ball 139

Cinnamon Basil Ice Cream 139

Peach Basil Lemonade Slush 141

Frozen Strawberry-Basil Margarita 141

Vegan Recipes with Herbs 142

Vegan Almond Cheese and Garlic Herb Spread ... 142

Zhoug Sauce 143

Parsley Dill Pesto 144

Quinoa Salad with Herbs 145

Rosemary Cauliflower Mash 146

Veggie and Herbs Burritos 146

Jackfruit, Mango, and Dill Salad 147

Baked Farro with Herbs and Tomatoes 148

Mango and Mint Smoothie 150

Rosemary and Tahini Cookies 150

Thyme and Raspberry Gin Cocktail 151

Conclusion 153

References 155

Introduction

"For roughly 2,000 years, Chinese herbalists have treated Malaria using a root extract, commonly known as chang shan, from a type of hydrangea that grows in Tibet and Nepal"(Delude, 2012).

Herbal medicines have been used for centuries to treat illnesses, from annual flu to chronic illness and autoimmune diseases. Historically, herbal medicines have been used to treat autoimmune diseases because many herbal practices believe that we need to heal the gut to heal any illness or disease. We need to change our diets and consume healthier foods, especially foods that have medicinal purposes, and our body's natural healing mechanisms will be boosted, and we will heal.

I know that it can be hard initially to believe in these remedies if you've grown up with conventional medicine. Did conventional medicine ever cure your diseases? Did you ever feel fully energized and happy after a conventional medical treatment? It can be hard to step out of the comfort of the known, but making the change to herbal medicine will have massive benefits.

I didn't believe in herbal medicines for over 20 years

because I had grown up with traditional Western medicinal practices. When I was sick, my parents would bring me to the doctors…. Which would prescribe me medication, but later in the year, I would feel sick again. However, I can openly say that transitioning into natural medicine was the proper cure for every ailment I had. Now I feel better than I've ever felt before.

I'm saving hundreds of dollars that I wasted on conventional medicine and doctors that would never really have the answer to cure my ailments. Health care is costly, and when you are experiencing chronic illnesses or pain, whether mental or physical, it can become expensive to visit the doctors, get new medications, and pay for them out of pocket.

When you transition from traditional western medicinal practices to herbal practices, you will see many positive changes in your life. You're going to wake up every morning fully energized and excited for the day because your body will be stronger and healthier than before. Our bodies aren't made to be inflamed, stiff, and slow – we're meant to have alkaline and strong bodies, ready to wake up every morning to give our best and enjoy life to the fullest. Medications also come with the possibility of nasty side effects that can leave you feeling unenergized and not like yourself.

It took me over 20 years to accumulate all the knowledge and experience I have now. Along my journey, I have helped people heal from illnesses that, for doctors, were not healable. I have seen transformations in people I never thought were possible until then. The number one thing I've learned on my journey is that everything is reversible and healable.

Growing your herbal garden will give you access to the many physical benefits and medicinal uses of herbs. But the act of gardening itself also has numerous physical and mental health benefits. Although it isn't super strenuous, gardening has many physical benefits, including improving lung and heart health, increasing hand strength, giving you a boost of vitamin D, reducing blood pressure, helping to maintain and lose weight, and can fight some cancers. The mental health benefits of gardening include decreasing depressive symptoms, lessening stress and anxiety, and improving overall mood.

Your life will change, and you will learn much as you continue reading this book. It's time to start learning how to create your herbal garden and save thousands of dollars.

Chapter 1: Gardening 101

Gardening has been around for thousands of years. After humanity evolved to form communities, there was a need for ensuring enough supplies for everyone, whether this was food or medicine. The ideas of gardening and farming came into existence. Looking back to ancient civilizations, there were no giant turbines or farming equipment, so farmers would need to use similar techniques to what we use for gardening today. Unlike today, ancient civilization depended not only on farmers to produce foods and goods such as medicine; individual families and communities would have their gardens and animals to create goods such as wool, meat, and vegetables.

In today's society, there are big pharmaceutical companies that create medications. Still, in ancient civilizations, physicians would have their gardens to grow medicinal herbs and experiment with what each herb could treat.

Despite the presence of farming communities and big farming companies, people still choose to grow their food for many reasons. You might produce your food to save money at the grocery store, or you are trying to go organic and want to avoid the pesticides and MSGs in certain foods found at the grocery store. Gardening can be heaps of fun and has numerous benefits for our mental and physical health. Many people garden as a hobby because of the benefits alone. However, gardening takes work and preparation. In this chapter, I will walk you through how to start a garden and what you need.

A Garden Requires Dedication and Consistency

Keeping any plant, whether this is a small cactus or an entire garden, requires dedication and consistency. Like humans, plants need some form of commitment and consistency when taking care of them. Let's look at the example of when we are exercising. When we are dedicated to exercising and being consistent with the amount of exercise we get, we will benefit more. The same goes for plants.

Any plant will thrive when you are consistent with how you care for it. The plant's environment is essential to the growth and health of the plant because it impacts the many different chemical reactions that must take place for the plant to live and grow. You must be consistent in numerous areas, such as lighting, water, fertilizer, and atmospheric conditions.

Fluctuations in temperatures are one of the biggest enemies to plant growth. When your plant is in an environment where the temperatures fluctuate unnaturally, it will not be able to grow. Yes, there will be changes in the temperature throughout the day and into the night, but they will be gradual and natural, allowing the plant to adapt. Maintaining one temperature in an outdoor garden is impossible. There will always be days that are hotter or colder than average. However, if you are planting during the right season and maintaining consistency in other areas, the plant will still be able to thrive.

Photosynthesis is the process in which plants turn light, water, and oxygen into carbohydrates or energy for them to grow. Light is critical for the health of a plant, and understanding the level of light that is needed will help you maintain a healthy plant. When you do not give your plants the proper amount of light or too much light, they will wilt and die. Indoor gardens can use artificial light to help boost exposure or even purchase lights specifically made for plants to help them grow. If you are using artificial lights, change them annually to ensure your plants are getting the most out of them.

Nutrient uptake and ensuring that your plants absorb all the nutrients they need rely on the soil's pH (potential hydrogen) levels. If you were growing a tomato plant, you would produce more tomatoes if you maintained a healthy pH level. When you are watching the pH levels of the soil and keeping them consistent, your plants will grow more and have a larger yield.

Consistency in the environment is only one area. You also need to be dedicated to all the work that comes with gardening. It is not a hobby you can just put to the side and forget about for months. Gardens need constant care, and you need to be dedicated to giving this care, or your plants will not survive. Whether you have one plant in a tiny indoor garden or have a large outdoor garden, you need to be dedicated and consistent with the care of the plants.

If you want to try and grow a lot of the food you are consuming but don't know where to start, the next section will discuss how you can create a backyard garden and all the necessary tools.

Starting a Backyard Garden

A backyard garden might sound like something extremely extravagant or needs lots of space, but in reality, it is entirely up to you how big you want your garden to be. Whether you live in a small town with a big backyard or in a city apartment with only a small balcony, you can have a garden. When starting a backyard garden, follow these steps:

1. **Know your climate zone.** Depending on where you live in the world, there will be plants that you can and cannot grow without the aid of a greenhouse. Each climate region will have suitable plants to grow in—understanding which ones will give you an idea of which ones you can have. Knowing your climate zone will also eliminate you from choosing a plant that will not survive.
2. **Choose the plants you want to grow.** After you know the climate region, you can choose the plants you want to grow. Reflect on the plants you are most likely to consume during this process. Don't grow a vegetable, fruit, or herb that you will not use in some capacity.
3. **Look at all possible locations and choose the best one.** The area of your garden is critical.

You need to consider how much sun exposure there is, how much shade or trees around will impact temperature, etc.

4. **If you already have an area with soil, test it.** If you have a backyard, test the soil. You can pay a fee to your local service office, who can test the ground and give you an outline of the components in the earth. This gives you an idea about any changes you need to make to ensure the soil is healthy.

5. **Buy essential gardening tools; you don't need anything fancy.** You do not need to go out and buy the most expensive gardening tools. Nor do you need to buy many tools. In the next section, I outline the essential gardening tools to buy.

6. **Create a garden bed.** A gardening bed is an area where you are clear of all vegetation. This is extremely easy for an indoor garden, but for a backyard garden, you will want to ensure that your area is completely clear of vegetation so that all your new plants will get the most nutrients they can. If you are using a part of your yard, you must remove all grass. After removing the grass, apply about four inches of compost onto the area.

7. **Choose between growing your plants from seeds or transplant seedlings.** When you start with seeds, it is a long process to get them growing and has many challenges. It can be easier for beginners to transplant seedlings, despite being slightly more expensive. If you choose to transplant

seedlings, make sure that you inspect the roots when buying and ensure that the plant is not root-bound (when the plant's roots become knotted and tight, not allowing for proper water absorption). This might mean it will not survive the transplant because it is already unhealthy.
8. **After choosing between seeds or seedlings, plant them carefully.** If you are sowing seeds, ensure they are at the appropriate depth and cover them with soil using your hand. Seedlings will be in nursery pots, and you will need to remove them carefully and carefully massage the soil and roots so that they are no longer stuck in the shape of a pot. This allows the plant to extend roots into the new soil easily. This is extremely important for root-bound plants.
9. **Water your plants.** The amount you water a plant is wholly based on the plant and season. However, plants need more water during the growing season, usually about an inch of water a week when there is no rain. You can check if the soil is damp enough by sticking your finger two inches into the soil. If the soil feels dry, it needs water.
10. **Cover soil with rocks and mulch.** Covering the soil with mulch or rocks makes it harder for weeds to grow. When there are fewer weeds, worms, and other organisms in the soil, it can thrive, allowing for more nutrients for the plants and healthier soil. Be sure to have suitable material for the right plants. Vegetables will thrive with

straw and leaves, while flowers and fruit will thrive with wood chips.
11. **Take care of your garden throughout the seasons.** The growing season is not the only time you need to take care of the garden. Different things need to be done each season. Summer is the growing season, and you will need to water your plants more. The fall season is clean-up time and prepping for winter, such as cutting off leaves that are wilting and dying. The springtime is for prep and ensuring that weeds are not growing. If you do not keep weeds at bay in the spring, they will only worsen in the summer.

Tools you will need for a backyard garden: gloves, pruning shears, trowel, angled shovel, garden rake, loppers (only if you need to clear large branches), garden fork, spade, hoe, garden hose, watering can or wand, and wheelbarrow (only if you need a large amount of soil, rocks, or mulch transported).

When looking at the store and looking at the tools, remember to think about the size of the garden. If you have a small garden on your balcony, you don't need a wheelbarrow, loppers, a shovel, or a garden hose. The tools you buy are entirely up to you and your space. Don't buy tools you do not need because they will take up room that you don't have if you live in an apartment.

Starting with Potting

When we think of gardening, thoughts of having a

house in a small town with a big backyard might come into your mind. But this reality is not everyone's. You might think that if you live in a city apartment, you won't be able to have a garden, but this is false! If you live in a city, this section will be critical because we will discuss plotting out your garden, the best potting mix to use since you won't have natural soil, everything you will need, and the steps to get started.

Tips to Start

If you live in the city, you will likely be creating something known as a container garden, where all your plants are in pots rather than planted into the ground. If you are looking to do this, here are some tips to consider before you get started:

1. **Have a list of everything that you need before buying plants.** This will make the process of planting and maintaining healthy plants easier as you will not be wondering what you need or

have to go out and buy more.
2. **Test how much light your plants will get.** Before you go out and buy plants, put a pot or bowl where you want the plants to go and track how much sunlight they will get. You can do this in multiple areas to evaluate the best spot for each plant.
3. **Make sure that all your containers have drainage holes.** When you have a traditional garden, the soil and other natural debris help to drain any excess water. When you have a container garden, there must be an area where the excess water will go. Drainage holes allow excess water to be drained and ensure proper moisture levels. When you do not have adequate drainage, it can cause the roots to be submerged in water which will cause them to rot.
4. **Buy nutrients.** Typical potting soil will not have all the nutrients your plants need, so you need to feed your plants with other nutrients to remain healthy.
5. **Keep the plant tag and always go back to it.** When you buy plants from a nursery, they will have a plant tag that tells you the amount of sun, water, and nutrients it will need and will tell you how big the plant will be.
6. **If you are planting multiple plants in one pot, ensure they all have the exact needs.** You don't want to be planting a low-light plant with a high-light plant because neither will be getting the proper amount of sunlight as you try to

accommodate one or the other. The same goes for water. Make sure that you are mixing plants with the exact needs.

7. **Remember that some plants will die even with all the love and care you can give.** When we are trying super hard to take care of plants, it can be frustrating and saddening when a plant dies. Remember that sometimes a plant will just die, no matter how much TLC (tender, love, and care) you give it.

8. **Make gradual changes.** Many plants are susceptible to abrupt changes, so it is essential to acclimate them. This means that you make incremental changes rather than abrupt ones. For example, start acclimating your indoor plants to the outdoors by putting them outside first for an hour and gradually increasing the length of time.

9. **Think about your lifestyle before picking which plants to grow.** Gardening can take much time out of your day, depending on the number of plants you have and the time you will need to care for them. If you have a busy life, getting plants that require less care will be the best for you.

10. **There are many ways to fill your pot, but remember that the more potting soil you have, the healthier your plants will be.** People will often pack their pots with packing peanuts or recycles them to make them lighter, but this only serves to dry out the soil quicker.

Best Potting Mix to Start Sowing Seeds

If you are creating a container garden and choosing to sow seeds rather than buy seedlings, you want to ensure that you have the best potting mix to ensure the plant will sprout. There are tons on the market that you can buy, but to ensure that you get the best potting mix for your seeds, you should consider making one.

You might be thinking that sowing seeds require a potting mix that is super high in nutrients, but this is false. Too many nutrients can harm seeds and seedlings that are incredibly delicate.

Measure each component by the volume of the pot that you are using. You want to start with two parts compost as the base. The compost will be responsible for gradually releasing nutrients for the plants. Break up the compost until it reaches a fine texture. Rehydrate coconut fiber if needed and add two parts. Add one part of perlite, which is necessary for air content. Mix all these ingredients, ensuring it is mixed well, and store them in a lidded container in a cool, dry area.

How to Sow Seeds

Sowing seeds can be complicated, but it can also be very fulfilling as you nurture a plant from seed to maturity. Here is an outline of everything you will need to sow your seeds.

What you will need:

- planting trays

- small containers
- potting mix or seed starter
- seeds
- labels
- tray covers or plastic bags
- marker
- glow light (optional)

Reading the Package of Seeds

When you are sowing seeds, you must read the package because it will give you all the information you need to properly sow the seeds and ensure the plant's health. The box will tell you the planting time, the temperature, how long it will take the plant to get to maturity, the soil needs, and the amount of water and sun the seeds need. Always keep the package at hand to refer back to it.

Step-by-Step Guide on How to Start

Follow these steps to get started sowing your seeds and creating your garden:

1. Dampen potting mix and put into containers or seed starting containers. The mixture should feel like a wrung-out sponge and have the same dampness. The containers should be about two-thirds filled.
2. Plant the seeds following the instructions on seed packages. Each type of plant will have different directions and needs, so be sure to

follow them.
3. After planting, cover the seeds with more potting mix. The amount of mixture that goes on top depends on the plant and will be stated on the seed package.
4. Water the seeds after planting. The soil is dampened but watering right after allows the top layer to remain damp and not dry out quickly. Use a spray bottle for tiny seeds.
5. Cover the containers with plastic lids or bags. This helps maintain humidity and moisture, which are vital for growing seeds. Keep the seeds in an area that is warm and has no drafts. The ideal temperature is about 65-70 degrees Fahrenheit, but this might differ from plant to plant.
6. Once you see the seedlings sprout, remove the plastic and put it in indirect light.
7. Keep the soil moist, not wet, or the seedling will rot.
8. Make sure your seedling is getting 12-18 hours of light.
9. When leaves start to form on the seedlings, start feeding your plants nutrients. You will want to use a water-soluble fertilizer and dilute it before adding it to the plants. Your fertilizer should be high in nitrogen and potassium.
10. Acclimate your plants to the outdoors. Do this by setting them outside in a sheltered and shady spot for a bit and doing this for up to two weeks, increasing the time every day. To this point,

they have been indoors and will need to gradually be introduced to the outdoor weather. If the outdoor temperature does not go below 50 degrees Fahrenheit at night, you can leave your plants outdoors uncovered after this acclimation period.

Types of Herb Gardens

There is a magnitude of reasons why you might be deciding to grow a garden, whether this is inside or not. One of the reasons you might be growing your food is to access foods you don't readily have, such as herbs. There are many types of herb gardens you can grow.

Bee Garden

A bee garden is a garden comprised of plants that are attractive to bees. These gardens will have bee balm, basil, chamomile, fennel, lemon balm, lavender, oregano, sage, and thyme. If you have an outdoor garden, this is great for the plants' health as bees will help to pollinate the plants.

Medieval Garden

A medieval garden comprises herbs and plants deemed needing protection within monasteries during the Middle Ages. These plants include chives, caraway, iris, lavender, marjoram, mint, roses, rosemary, Santolina, and southernwood.

Shakespeare Garden

A Shakespeare garden is described as the non-poisonous garden depicted in Shakespeare's work. Common plants associated with these gardens include bay, carnation, hyssop, lavender, lemon balm, mustard, parsley, rosemary, strawberry, and thyme.

Indoor Herb Garden

Indoor herb gardens are perfect for someone who wants all-year-round access to fresh herbs. The most popular herbs indoors include basil, chives, dill, lavender, lemon verbena, mint, oregano, rosemary, sage, and thyme.

Gray and Silver Garden

Most people do not plant these gardens anymore, but they are an old English tradition. Plants in gray and silver gardens include applemint, gray lavender cotton, horehound, sage, silver thyme, and yarrow.

Fragrance Garden

Fragrance gardens are more about delighting the senses rather than being used for food consumption. Plants in a fragrance garden include bergamot, chamomile, geraniums, jasmine, mint, pineapple sage, southernwood, thyme, and sweet woodruff.

The type of garden you grow is entirely up to you and your needs. If you want a garden that provides fresh herbs all year round, you will want to produce an indoor herb garden.

Permaculture

Gardening might seem like a cut-and-dry activity you perform yourself, but many different groups and cultures are associated with gardening. Permaculture is one of many you will join when you join the gardening community. Permaculture "is the conscious design and maintenance of agriculturally productive ecosystems which have the diversity, stability, and resilience of natural ecosystems" (The Permaculture Research Institute, n.d.). Permaculture is the mutually beneficial integration of people and the environment, allowing us to sustainably acquire energy, shelter, food, and other needs from the earth. When we leave the realm of sustainability, we are no longer a part of permaculture. A personal garden is a tiny part of permaculture. A more prominent example would be the large farming companies.

Permaculture is a set of systems meant to model natural ecosystems to create sustainable agriculture systems, such as farming. These models are intended to exclude all external manipulation, including chemical fertilizers.

History of Permaculture

The term permaculture was coined by Bill Mollison and David Holmgren in the 1970s. The term is a contraction of the words permanent and agriculture. Permaculture was created at the peak when scientists began to understand the impact that even the most minor local action can have on the more extensive ecosystem. Before the creation of permaculture theory, other scientists, including Rachel Carson, looked at how human actions impacted the larger ecosystem, specifically chemical pesticides. Carson's research was on how chemical pesticides that were meant to keep insects and other pests from destroying crops had a more significant negative impact on the toxicity of the environment.

Rudolf Steiner

Rudolf Steiner (1861-1925) was a scientist and philosopher that created a biodynamic approach to agriculture. During his career, Steiner made observations of the impacts that humanity had on earth and concluded that without any change, western civilization would be destructive and would have irrevocable effects on the planet. Steiner's solution was that western societies needed to become aware of the connections between the physical and spiritual worlds. Carson was not the first person to write and talk about the impact of pesticides and chemicals on the earth. Steiner also noted the adverse effects that they would have.

Biodynamic agriculture is a combination of farming and religious-philosophical practices. This form of farming is meant to encompass all the more minor aspects of the whole, including the universe, the community you live in, other farmers, the animals, and the crops you grow.

Understanding Permaculture and Biodynamic Farming

Permaculture and biodynamic farming are similar as they both aim to exclude the use of external inputs such as chemical pesticides. You can think about biodynamic agriculture as a method of agriculture that goes beyond organic. Biodynamic farming practices also reject intensive farming methods. This farming method is meant to be as natural as possible with only a limited amount of human input.

Permaculture rejects using chemicals or anything that will harm the ecosystem, but they still use intensive farming methods. Permaculture can be organic farming but does not necessarily need to be. A permaculture is an approach that adopts ecological sciences, while biodynamic farming takes a more metaphysical approach.

There are permaculture gardens worldwide, but one of the best-known herbal gardens adopting permacultural ideas is Auroville in India.

Greenhouses

Some countries do not have the proper climate to grow different plants, fruits, and vegetables. Depending on your ecosystem, you cannot grow plants throughout the year. This is where greenhouses become a very vital part of farming and gardening.

Greenhouses are structures made of glass or plastic sheeting that allow plants to absorb sunlight but trap the heat that plants emit when they convert sunlight into energy. Greenhouses are excellent resources to have when you live in a colder climate because they can allow you to grow plants all year round while also opening up to planting options. However, like anything, greenhouses come with pros and cons.

The advantages of having a greenhouse include:

- You can make more money by being able to grow all year round.
- Stability and increase in yields.
- Allows for optimal conditions as they give protection from storms, invasive plant species, animals, and droughts.
- Can grow exotic plants.

The disadvantages of having a greenhouse include:

- It costs a lot of money to build a greenhouse, and you will need expert help.
- A lot of background knowledge is required to successfully grow plants in a greenhouse.
- Plants cannot be pollinated naturally while in a greenhouse.
- It can have high operational costs.
- Takes up much space.
- Pests can still enter and ruin crops if a greenhouse is set up wrong.

How to Start a Greenhouse

After building a greenhouse, you have to think about

where you will start. Growing plants in a greenhouse can be very difficult, so you will want to learn with the most accessible plants. Try growing peas, onion, tomatoes, potatoes, garlic, radishes, lettuce, sunflowers, and mushrooms when you start.

Tools you will need for greenhouse gardening include a hand trowel, fork, spade, pruning shears, hoe, gardening gloves, shovel, wheelbarrow, saw, and rake.

It is up to you which type of seeds you choose, whether these are seeds from a pack or seedlings. If you decide to work with seeds packages, you want to ensure that you write down the type of seeds and when you planted them. Also, make sure that you are keeping each package of seeds. If you are planting numerous plants, be extra careful when tracking when you planted each and when you water them. Starting a greenhouse can be very difficult, and you must be mindful of temperature control, light, and watering.

A greenhouse can become too hot, so you must be mindful of having windows and vents. Also, ensure that you have a temperature gauge on hand to know when to open and close windows and vents. During the winter, you need to make the days last longer so that your plants get the right amount of sunlight, so you will want to ensure that you have lights that will give your plants the boost they need. Watering is essential, so you need to watch for the signs you have over or underwatered your plants. Signs that your plants need more or less water include yellowing or super dry leaves or roots and overly dry or soggy soil. Depending on the greenhouse, you might have a watering system on a timer or watering your plants yourself. Always refer back to the seed packet to know how much you need to water your plants and if you are using a watering system, make sure you are planting things that need the same amount of water.

Water and Drainage Outdoor Gardens

Watering and ensuring you have proper drainage is different for indoor or outdoor gardens. Indoor and container gardens need constant observation and watering. You have to ensure that the moisture level of your soil is good and that the water is draining so that it is not sitting at the bottom of the pot. Check the dryness of the soil by poking your finger into the soil by a few inches. Outdoor gardens already have sufficient drainage with the soil, rocks, and mulch that you might use. Watering your outdoor garden can also be tricky because you must note the weather you have been experiencing. If you keep a watering schedule, make sure that you keep track of how much rain you are getting. If you have a week where you get much rain, you will want to skip watering your plants that week or reduce the amount you are watering them.

Organic Gardening

Depending on your health or your view of food, you might want to start eating primarily organic foods, but this can be hard to come by in regular grocery stores. This is when you might want to start organic gardening or the process of gardening without the use of synthetic pesticides or fertilizers. Essentially organic gardening is gardening with only the help of nature. One of the most significant benefits of organic gardening is that your natural resources are replenished as you continue to grow foods organically.

To start organic gardening, follow these steps:

1. Prepare the soil by adding organic matter to the soil. The longer you prepare your soil, the healthier your plants will be.
2. Create good compost. It might seem like compost is compost, but there is good and bad compost. You can create compost using kitchen

scraps, grass trimmings, and leaves. You can also buy compost.
3. Prepare the garden area but do not destroy the soil.
4. Select the right plants. Make sure you look at the climate area and choose the appropriate plants. When buying seeds and seedlings, ensure they are not prepared and grown with synthetic pesticides and chemicals.
5. Plant your crops.
6. Water your plants.
7. Remove any weeds that start to grow.
8. Providing nutrients to your garden by promoting the inclusion of healthy insects such as bees and plants will help boost nutrients while not competing for light, water, and nutrition. Use organic fertilizers to make up for what you cannot naturally increase. Organic fertilizers include agricultural lime, wood ash, rock phosphates, and manure.

There are so many options for starting a garden; you just need to think about your options and choose which path you want to go down.

Before you move on to the next chapter, do this small exercise: reflect on your life and think about why you want to start a garden and the amount of time and money you are willing to spend to maintain your garden. On average, the cost of starting a garden, no matter the type of plant you are growing, is very small. There is the upfront cost of buying any tools you might need, and in some cases, you might be able to use another person's or even have some lying around the house. You will also have to buy the seeds or seedlings you want to grow. On average, a packet of seeds is about three dollars, which is on the high end. Seedlings can range in price, but they are inexpensive when you compare them to the product you will have in the long run. At most, you will spend a hundred dollars or so to start your garden.

Medicinal herbs are on the rise as people try organic and natural alternatives to modern medicine. Compare the low and cost-effective prices of starting a garden to the hundreds, if not thousands, of dollars you might spend a month on medication. Starting to grow your medicinal herbs is a great way to save money while also getting the health benefits you need.

Understanding your reason for wanting to garden and the time you are putting in makes it much easier to plan what you need to get and how to plan your day with gardening. Planning your garden before executing it will make it much easier to follow through and allow you to choose which kind of garden to have. In the next chapter, we will talk about what makes the perfect space for your garden.

Chapter 2: The Perfect Space

You can do everything to keep your plants alive, but if you don't have the proper environment, your plants aren't going to be healthy. Before you start a garden, you need to look at the environment you have, whether this is indoors or outdoors. You will want to walk around your house or yard and note the areas you think will be the best for the garden you want to create. When considering which areas will be better suited, remember that different plants need different light, water, nutrients, and exposure levels.

Before you start a garden, you need to know all the tools and elements of your garden, such as soil, exposure, and location. This chapter will explain how to get to know your soil, optimize it, the different types of exposures your plants will go through, and the best geographical location to grow herbs.

Soil

Soil is the foundation of your garden. Without the proper soil, your plants will not survive, no matter all the TLC you give them. Think of soil as the utensil in which a plant eats. If a plant needs to be eating with a spoon, eating with a fork will not provide a suitable mechanism for getting nutrients into the organism. Ensuring the proper soil will allow your plant to get the most nutrients and water. The soil you have will also impact the plant's roots and ability to move and grow.

Properly chosen soil is going to:

- provide proper access to water, nutrients, and air
- boosts the plant's resistance to diseases and pests
- stabilizes roots

Knowing your soil is incredibly important for the health of your plants. It can be hard to recognize the type of soil you have at home, so you can always hire someone to test it to ensure you know the type, the pH, and any toxins that might damage your plants. The seed packets or the plant cards in seedlings will often tell you the kind of soil that you need for each plant. You can also ask someone at a plant nursery about which soil would be best for your garden.

There are numerous soil types, and each plant will require a different kind of soil. If your plant is not in suitable soil, it will not be able to absorb the water and nutrients that it needs adequately.

There are six main types of soil that you will want to consider when looking into different plants, including:

- **Loamy soil** is characterized by being slightly damp and fine-textured. This soil is best for gardening, shrubs, and lawns because it holds many nutrients, has good drainage, and retains moisture. This soil warms quickly in the spring, but it does not dry out quickly in the summer because of its ability to hold water.
- **Sandy soil** is characterized by feeling gritty, drying fast, holding few nutrients, and warming more quickly. Most herbs need as many nutrients as possible, especially if you are regularly harvesting so you want soil that will hold nutrients.

- **Peaty soil** is characterized by feeling damp and spongy, holding fewer nutrients, warming fast in the spring, but retaining much water and requiring more drainage. Many herbs prefer moist soil but nothing soggy or spongy.
- **Clay soil** is characterized by poor draining, warming up slowly, and being sticky when wet and hard when dry. This soil can hold many nutrients when drainage is optimized. The poor draining of clay makes roots prone to rotting.
- **Chalky soil** is characterized by having many stones and draining efficiently. Chalky soil is alkaline and can lead to yellow leaves and stunted growth because of a lack of nutrients and too much draining.
- **Silty soil** is characterized by being very rich in nutrients, holding moisture, and feeling soapy and soft. Organic matter like compost is needed to improve drainage. After loamy soil, silty is your best bet.

Soil pH

Soil is naturally acidic or alkaline, which can affect the growth of a plant. A soil's pH is essential to the health of a plant. A soil's acidity or alkalinity is measured with pH values or "a measure of hydrogen ion concentration" (Queensland Government, 2013). PH levels are measured on a scale of 1-14, with high pH levels being alkaline and low pH levels being acidic. On average, soil falls between 3.5-10, with soil in rainy areas ranging from 5-7 and 6.5-9 in dryer areas. A neutral soil will have a pH level of 6.5-7.5, while an alkaline soil will be over 7.5. Acidic soil will have a pH level of 5.5-6.5, and anything lower than 5.5 is considered strongly acidic. A soil pH between 8.5-10 is alkaline, and between 10-14 is highly alkaline.

The pH levels of soil affect a plant's ability to absorb nutrients because it impacts the solubility of chemicals and nutrients. Most nutrients that a plant needs are at their optimal levels in neutral soil.

Acidic soil is much more harmful to plants than alkaline as it can cause a magnitude of issues, including:

- low levels of molybdenum and phosphorus, which are essential nutrients for plant growth
- magnesium and calcium deficiency
- manganese and aluminum toxicity

The pH level of your soil is not permanent; you can change it by optimizing your soil naturally, which I will tell you how to do in the next section.

How to Optimize Your Soil Naturally

If you find that your plants are not thriving no matter the care you are giving them, this might mean that there is an issue with the soil. Optimizing your soil to provide the plant with the most benefits possible might solve your plant's declining health. There are numerous ways to optimize your soil, but first, consider getting a test done on your soil's pH level. The results of this test can tell you what is wrong with the soil and give you a direction of where to go.

Composting is one of the best ways to optimize your soil naturally, but first, here are some other options:

- Put mulch on the soil surface.
- Do not step in your garden too much to reduce soil compaction. When making your garden, consider making it a size that will allow you to reach the center from either side so that you do not need to walk through it.
- Rotate where you put plants each year. Rotating them will help to reduce nutrient deficiency in the soil. Putting one plant in the same spot every year deprives the soil of nutrients other plants can give it.
- To protect the soil, grow cover crops such as broadleaf greens, radishes, kale, and turnips.
- Add organic matter, such as manure, to the soil.

Composting

Composting is the process of turning organic matter scraps, such as kitchen scraps and leaves, into enriching fertilizer for your plants. Composting works by speeding up the decomposition process by promoting the presence of fungi, bacteria, worms, and sowbugs. Once the organic matter is decomposed, it is now garden soil enriched with nutrients and perfect for your garden.

You can buy compost, but it is fulfilling to create your compost, and it has numerous benefits, including conserving water, reducing food waste, and reducing methane emissions. But how exactly do you make compost?

First, you will want to invest in a composter. A composter will help the whole composting process and help reduce unhealthy organisms and pests from entering the compost mix.

The best compost needs to have the correct carbon to nitrogen ratio. You want to have a lot more carbon-infused items than nitrogen-infused ratio. The ideal carbon to nitrogen ratio is one-third green products (nitrogen-rich) and two-thirds brown products (carbon-rich). When your compost pile has too much nitrogen, you will find that it smells terrible. Adding more carbon-rich materials will help alleviate this and get your compost more balanced. Never have nitrogen-rich material on top of the pile. Always cover it with carbon-rich ones to lessen the smell.

Carbon-rich organic matter includes dried leaves, branches, pieces of wood, sawdust, brown paper bags shredded, coffee grounds and filters, eggshells, corn stalks, peels, conifer needles, wood ash, and peat moss. Nitrogen-rich organic matter includes food scraps, kitchen waste, manures, green lawn clippings, and green leaves.

Things that you should not compost include:

- bones, meat, and fish scraps (unless you use a composter)
- unwashed fruit peels because they commonly have pesticide residue
- pet manure

- diseased plants and weeds
- black walnut leaves

Exposure

If you have an outdoor garden, your plants will constantly be exposed to something. Wind and sun exposure are the most common exposures that you need to worry about. However, your plants can be exposed to more depending on where you live and the climate.

Wind Exposure

No matter where you live, your plants will be exposed to high winds. Although wind is needed for pollination, persistent high winds are detrimental to a plant's health. A plant could yield up to 50% less if high winds are constant. Imagine the leaf of a plant as skin. There are pores or stomata on a plant's leaves that can be opened and closed and allow for water to be absorbed and allow the plant to breathe. When a plant is experiencing high winds, it will close these stomata to prevent water loss. But when these pores are closed, the plant cannot breathe as well, leading to slower growth.

Do not fear, however, because there are multiple ways that you can windproof your garden, including:

- Protect your garden by clearing any debris that could damage plants or securing them where they are if they cannot be moved.
- Prune or cut any overhanging branches.

- Create a long-term windproofing plan, such as planting hedges or considering a greenhouse.
- Prepare plants such as climbing ones for high wind by securing them.

Sun Exposure

Sunlight is essential to plant growth, but prolonged sun exposure can harm a plant's health. The seed packet or plant card on a seedling will tell you the amount of sun a plant needs. This can be partial sun, full sun, or full shade. Full sun means at least 6-8 hours of sun, partial sun means about 4-6 hours, and full shade means little to no direct sun exposure. You need to ensure that you are providing the correct sun exposure because a plant that requires full shade will not survive exposure to the sun.

When a plant gets too little light, the leaves will start to yellow as it is not getting enough energy and food from the sun. Too much heat and the sun will cause the plant to become dehydrated, and leaves will yellow, curl, and fall off.

The Best Exposure for a Garden

The direction your garden is facing is essential to the amount of exposure that your garden will get. Choosing where you will plant should reflect the plant's light needs. If they need full sun, aim for them to be in the sunlight right in the morning as the afternoon sun is hotter and can cause heat damage. If you live in the Northern Hemisphere, plant your garden on the south side of your property to give the most sunlight. If you can't do this, the east or west side of the property should be your next option.

Suppose you are planting a vegetable garden in rows from north to south so that they are all equally exposed to sunlight. If you are planting more than one plant, be mindful of spacing and height so that some plants don't shadow others.

The Best Geographical Location to Grow Herbs

Herbs are some of the most common plants that are grown at home. They can be grown both indoors and outdoors. The advantages of indoor herb gardens include easy access, they can grow all year round, and you do not need to weed. The benefits of outdoor herb gardens include more space, higher yields, and more flavorful plants.

It is entirely up to you if you decide to grow an indoor or outdoor garden. An indoor herb garden should be placed in southwestern facing windows or a corner with south and west-facing windows to get optimal light. An outdoor herb garden needs about 6-8 hours of sunlight a day with loam soil that will drain well. Manure, peat moss, or compost is recommended to improve the soil.

After you have decided on the areas best suited for your garden, draw a map of the area. Draw a garden layout and note where you will get the most sun and wind exposure. After you have noted this, write down which plants will thrive in particular garden areas. This map will allow you to plan where you will plant each to go and will enable you to provide the proper amount of light, exposure, nutrient, and water. If your garden is indoors, write down the different rooms you have, the amount of light it will get, and the temperature. Create a list of plants that will be best suited in each room.

As you can see from this and the last chapter, there is much planning to start a garden. Understanding the basics we have discussed should be your first step, and then deciding which plants you want and where to plant them. Now that you know the basics, we can start talking about how you can have your garden blooming all year round. In the next chapter, we are going to talk about everything planting.

Fun Fact: You take care of plants, and they take care of you. Keeping plants in the house helps to purify the air, making it better for you, keeping plants is a big stress reliever!

Chapter 3: Planting

After the planning phase, it's time to start the hands-on garden, like actually planting your plants. This step is the make-or-break-it moment. If you don't plant your seeds or seedlings correctly, they will not survive, and your garden will never sprout. This chapter will talk about all things planting, including indoor and outdoor, the difficulties, mistakes to avoid, which herbs are easy, and the many ways to plant your herbs.

The Importance of Buying Organic Seeds

Before you even start planting, you must think about the seeds you buy. Although you might not be going for a completely organic garden, it is essential to buy organic seeds. But first, what exactly constitutes an organic seed? Organic is not a label producers can just slap onto their products; instead, they need to meet specific requirements and be certified organic. Like organic gardening or farming, organic seeds are produced and collected with the same techniques, meaning there are no synthetic treatments or means of collection. Organic does not imply any chemicals. There are natural producers that organic farmers use, but they are natural and not harmful to the environment or your body, like synthetic chemicals.

When shopping for seeds, you will see labels that say organic or treated seeds. Treated seeds are covered in a coating to reduce how quickly the seed will rot in the soil. Beans and peas have seeds very susceptible to rotting in the earth, so they will often be sold as treated seeds. When handling these seeds, always wash your hands and never eat the seeds. If any residue of this coating is left after the seeds have been grown, it will be very little on the food you are harvesting and is entirely safe for consumption.

Organic and treated seeds are no different in how they will grow. When a plant is grown organically, the seeds do not change genetically, causing them to have bigger yields. Instead, buying organic seeds versus those treated can be about your mindset of what you put into your body.

Often, treated seeds will cost more than organic because of the cost to treat seeds. Organic seeds will save you more money and support local organic farmers since organic seeds will need to be sold near where they were collected. Supporting local businesses can help increase access to organic foods and help farmers and the community. The biggest reason you should buy organic seeds is to support local farmers. Organic seeds do not produce healthier plants, bigger yields, or even better-tasting foods. It's more about growing and buying organically to benefit the earth and the farmers around you.

Planting Seeds

The tricky part of gardening is understanding how to plant seeds. Each plant species will have different specifications, which can change depending on whether you are growing your plants indoors or outdoors.

When planting indoors, follow these steps:

1. Use sterile seed starting mix; if you do not have access to this, use a soilless mix. Using these options will significantly reduce the risk of introducing diseases to the seeds. These options are also optimal for root growth because they are light and fluffy, allowing movement.
2. Do not sow a seed too deep or too shallow. Seed packets will specify how deep they need to be sown.
3. Be consistent with moisture levels. Seeds need moisture to germinate; consistent with this will give the best results. Once a seed germinates, be sure to check it regularly. If the leaves are rigid,

the plant does not need water; if they are wilting, they do.
4. Use heating mats to keep temperatures at around 70-80 degrees F. Temperature is essential for keeping moisture levels up.

It is your choice to sow seeds indoors or not, but when deciding, make sure that you consider the seed's size. If your plant has a tiny seed, it might be best to grow this indoors because it can get lost and not germinate in your garden. After it has grown in size, you can move it outside. You can also plant indoors all year round, so if you want, you could start growing vegetables early and then move them outside to get a jump on the season.

When planting outdoors, follow these steps:

1. Know when you can plant. Make sure you are not planting too early or late. Depending on your seeds, they will need to be planted at different times.
2. Prepare the garden by adding organic matter and mixing it with the soil. If you need, loosen about a foot deep worth of soil.
3. Weeds will always be present in an outdoor garden, so clear them before planting.
4. Add fertilizer to make up for any soil deficiencies that might be present.
5. Plant seeds following the directions on the packet. Start slow-growing plants such as tomatoes, cauliflower, and peppers indoors, then move outdoors. Plant your seeds in rows and give them an appropriate amount of space.
6. Ensure good contact between the seed and soil by firming the soil with your hands.
7. Use a fine mist to water the garden. A full-power stream from a hose can disrupt the spot where the seeds sit and push them together.
8. Add a thin layer of mulch to the garden to stop the soil from crusting and entrapping the seeds.
9. Mark each row and where you planted the seeds. This helps you know what a plant is and what a weed is.
10. Keep the soil moist. Seeds can dry out very quickly, especially when it is windy.

Difficulties You May Encounter When Planting Seeds

There will always be difficulties when you are working with plants. Whether you are a beginner or have been gardening for over half of your life. You will always experience problems that you will have to think around.

Common difficulties that you might encounter while planting seeds include:

- poor germination
- seedlings yellowing
- seedlings dying
- tall and spindly growth

Poor germination can occur for numerous reasons, including insufficient water or moisture, too low or too high temperatures, and seeds planted too deep. When seedlings start to yellow, that means they have inadequate nutrients. If this is not corrected, it will lead to the seedlings dying. If you are growing plants indoors, you might encounter the problem of tall and spindly growth for numerous reasons, including not enough light, too high of a temperature, too much watering, too much fertilizer, and crowded conditions.

You can prevent many of these challenges by avoiding some of the most common mistakes that any person is starting to garden makes. Common mistakes include:

- not reading the seed packet - not making this mistake can stop you from making nearly all the

others on this list
- not planting seeds at the right time
- not having seeds at the right temperature
- watering your seeds too much or too little
- using the wrong seed starting mix or soil
- using too much or too little fertilizer
- not adapting your indoor plants to the outdoors (also known as the hardening process) before moving them outside
- planting your seeds in the wrong pots
- not having enough or having too much light

Planting from Division and What Is It?

This might sound surprising, but sowing seeds or planting seedlings is not the only way to start planting your garden. There are various planting methods, and the first one we will discuss is planting from division. This means that while a plant is dormant, you will dig it up, separate the roots into different plants and replant them separately. Meaning you can grow more herbs without needing to start from scratch. Division should only occur when the plant is dormant and at least two years old. If you try to divide a plant when it is actively growing or too young, the experience of digging the plant up and separating the roots can cause the plant to die. The dormant season for plants is in early spring and late fall.

Follow these steps to plant from division:

1. Look for the plants growing in clumps, such as

chives, mint, and tarragon. Plants in clusters are the best choice for division.
2. Dig up the entire plant, ensuring you are gentle and not severing any roots.
3. After the entire plant is out, untangle as many roots as possible, separating the cluster into smaller bunches. Once you have separated the plant into smaller groups, cut any roots keeping them attached.
4. Replant the divided bunches into your garden or pots.
5. Water your plants so that the roots do not dry out.

Herbs that are easy to grow from division include tarragon, rhubarb, strawberries, marjoram, mint, oregano, thyme, chives, and lovage.

Planting from Cuttings and What Is It?

Another method of planting is to plant from cuttings. This method is similar to planting from division but with a few extra steps. It means cutting a stem from the plant and placing it in water to form a new set of roots. After the roots form, you can replant the plant. Follow these steps to plant from cuttings successfully:

1. If your plant has a stem, cut it about a quarter of an inch below a root node. They look like small protrusions along the stem.
2. Place the cutting into a glass and fill room temperature water until the root node is covered.

Place the cup in indirect light.
3. Keep the same water for about three to five days, then change it. Rinse the roots and plant off every time you switch the water out. When propagating like this, the plant and roots can form a film that should be gently wiped away.
4. Keep in water until the plant starts to form roots. This can take weeks or months.
5. When the roots are three to five inches long, replant them into a pot with soil.

Not all plants can be propagated from cuttings. Houseplants and herbs are the most common plants with which you will find success. Herbs that are easy to grow from cutting include basil, mint, oregano, thyme, sage, lavender, rosemary, and savory.

Potting

Growing any plant indoors comes with the extra step of planting into a pot or potting. Because you are growing a plant inside or do not have access to a garden bed, there needs to be a spot where you can plant your herbs or seedling. Depending on the plant, you might plant a few or have one plant in one pot. Clay and terracotta pots are recommended, and make sure that they have adequate drainage.

Steps to potting your seedlings:
1. After you have bought pots for your seedlings, soak them in water if they are clay or terracotta. These types of pots are moisture-wicking so

soaking them before potting your plants ensures that the soil will not dry out as quickly.
2. Mix in compost, approximately one cup for a six-inch pot, and soilless mix (as discussed in an earlier chapter) or with potting soil. Fill the pot so that it is an inch below the top of the pot.
3. Make a planting hole in the soil, remove the seedling from its nursery pot, and put it in the soil.
4. If the soil around the seedling's roots is compact and dry, massage the soil gently to loosen it up.
5. If you are planting more than one plant into one pot, repeat the process of creating planting holes and inserting plants.
6. Water the plants thoroughly, ensuring that the water is draining correctly.

Repotting

Repotting is the process of moving a plant from its old pot to a new pot. As plants grow, they will outgrow their pots, like how we outgrow our clothes. Common reasons why you might need to repot your plants include:

- Your plant needs more space. You will be able to see this if roots are starting to grow out of the drainage holes.

- Replace old soil with new and better quality. Repotting allows you to give your plant the refreshment it needs. After a time, your soil will lose its nutrients and need to be replaced to provide the plant with a better environment.

- As we discussed earlier, you might be unpotting and repotting a plant to divide the roots.
- You might also decide that you want to change the aesthetic of your plants. This is the least recommended reason to repot your plants as it can cause the plant to go into shock and die. If you want to improve aesthetics, you can put your plant's pot inside a slightly bigger one.

It can be hard to recognize when your plant needs to be repotted, so here are some of the most common signs:

- roots growing out of drainage holes, as we said before
- soil looks like its disintegrating or is extremely dry
- water is not absorbed and sits on top of the soil
- the plant seems way too big for the pot

Follow these steps to repot your plants:

1. Get a bigger pot than the current one your plant is in. Your new pot should be at least one inch bigger and deeper than the previous one.
2. Use a coffee filter or other porous material to cover the drainage hole. These materials allow water to pass through but prevent soil from falling out.
3. Add in new soil, creating a base for the plant to sit on. Make sure it isn't too high, or the plant will spill out.
4. Before removing your plant from the old pot,

water it to ensure it stays healthy through the repotting process.
5. Place your hand on the pot and turn it upside down to remove the plant. Do not pull the plant out, as it could damage it. If it doesn't slip out immediately, try twisting it in either direction a few times. If this doesn't work, try a knife to separate the soil from the pot.
6. Untangle and prune the rootball gently.
7. Place the plant into the new pot, pressing it into the base layer of soil. Make sure it is centered, and add soil. Pat down the soil, ensuring the plant is secure. Water the plant to help settle the soil.

Potting different herbs into one pot can be beneficial for saving space and can be relatively harmless for the plants if they are compatible with one another. If you must plant different plants together, make sure you pick herbs with the same light, water, nutrient, and temperature needs. When you plant incompatible herbs together in a single pot, it can cause one or both to die as they are getting too much or too little of the water, sunlight, or nutrients.

Herbs you can plant together include:

- Mediterranean herbs including sage, thyme, marjoram, rosemary, and lavender
- moisture-loving herbs, including parsley and basil
- lemon-scented herbs, including lemon thyme and lemon verbena
- mints such as catmint, spearmint, orange mint,

peppermint, and lemon balm

Herbs to avoid planting together include:

- sage with onions and cucumbers
- wormwood and fennel around any other plant
- dill and anise with carrots
- dill with tomatoes
- alliums such as garlic with peas and beans
- rue with basil, sage, and cabbage

Why Should Certain Herbs Not Be Planted Together?

Incompatible needs are only one reason you won't want to plant certain plants in the same pot or near each other in the garden. Depending on the herbs you are growing, if you plant two that don't work together, it can cause them to taste differently. Certain herbs are powerful, and when planted with others, they can affect the taste of the plants around them, not in a good way.

Some herbs are just bad neighbors and will kill the other herbs when planted next to others. Herbs that don't get along can also cause stunted growth to occur. Fennel is an excellent example of this. It is a powerful herb and not a good garden neighbor as it impacts the development of the herbs around it, and if there is a lot, it can be deadly. However, fennel benefits a garden as it attracts aphid-eating insects, promoting better garden health. If you are planting fennel in your garden, keep it on the edges, or go even further and put it in containers.

How to Start a Small Herbal Permaculture Garden

Medicinal herbs are some of the best and easiest herbs to grow and can save you tons of money down the line by reducing how much food you are buying at the grocery store and can reduce medical costs. Growing medicinal herbs is a great way to introduce permaculture into your life because it is sustainable, helps improve the environment, and allows you to create at-home remedies.

When considering creating an herbal permaculture garden, you need to think about the three permaculture zones:

- Zone one is reserved for the herbs and plants you frequently harvest. This zone is often called the kitchen top herb garden. You will grow herbs you are going to use often.
- Zone two is reserved for your small vegetable garden. This is for plants such as fruits and vegetables that take longer to grow and won't be harvested as much as the herbs in zone one. Growing some herbs in your outdoor garden can help promote the health of your garden.
- Zone three is a larger area where you can grow larger plants such as medicinal herbs and mints. Instead, it is the larger area where you can grow larger plants and be outreached to larger plants and even wild ones. If you are not giving others some plants, you can transform them into compost.

Herbs you can grow in your permaculture herbal garden

include rosemary, parsley, garlic, peppermint, lemon balm, dandelion, chamomile, chickweed, and lavender. Remember that zone two is also designated for vegetables and fruits you might want to grow. Consider which herbs will pair well with any other plants you want.

You will want to adopt the permaculture principles when creating a permaculture garden. The 12 permaculture principles you need to know are:

1. Observe than interact.
2. Catch and store energy.
3. Collect your yield.
4. Regulate yourself and take feedback.
5. Understand the value of renewable resources and services and use them.
6. Reduce all waste.
7. Take a step back and look at the bigger picture.
8. Do not segregate plants.
9. Look at solutions that will have an impact in the long run.
10. Use diversity in your garden.
11. Use spaces that are overlooked.
12. Respond to change creatively.

Now you know everything about how to plant your garden, no matter where you are putting your garden. But, after planting, you can't just leave your plants to grow. You must maintain them, or they are going to die. Learning to maintain your herbal garden is essential for keeping it flourishing and blooming all year round. Maintaining your garden will ensure you can harvest your medical herbs all year round and treat your ailments. In the next chapter, we will discuss everything you need to know about maintaining your herbal garden.

Before we move on to the next chapter, let's do a small quiz. How often do you need to maintain your garden?

    a. Everyday
    b. Every other day
    c. Once a week
    d. Every few weeks

Choose an answer before moving on to the next chapter, where you will learn just how frequently you need to maintain and monitor your garden.

Chapter 4: Maintaining

You are starting an herb garden which likely means you want to harvest your herbs and other plants for years to come. An indoor garden will give you year-round harvesting possibilities, while an outdoor will only give you seasonal harvests. However, even though you are only going to use your outdoor garden seasonally, you need to maintain it all year round to ensure that you can continue to grow plants the following year. Maintaining your garden, whether indoors or outdoors, is vital for the health of your plants and ensures that you can harvest your plants year after year. This chapter will discuss the many ways to maintain your garden and keep it beautiful and thriving.

The Importance of Maintaining Your Herb Garden

There is no such thing as a garden that does not need maintenance. Depending on your garden type, more care might be required, but your plants will always need to be maintained to survive. Indoor gardens will require slightly less maintenance than outdoor gardens because you will not need to winterize your plants.

Herb gardens, especially ones filled with low-maintenance herbs, do not need much maintenance. Ensuring your plants have the proper sunlight, water, and soil will keep your garden healthy and flourishing.

Setting up your garden and then not maintaining it will cause your plants to die, and you won't be able to reap the benefits of gardening and the medicinal properties of the herbs. There is no point in starting a garden if you don't maintain it from the beginning because you won't be able to harvest your herbs. Maintaining your herbs should become a habit to ensure you get all the benefits from your garden.

Ensuring that your plants have healthy soil and the proper amount of sunlight is only one of the many ways you can maintain your garden. Maintenance of your garden includes watering, trimming, pruning, and staking your herbs.

Watering Your Herbs

The first way you need to maintain your herbs is to water them. Depending on the plant, you will need to water them with different amounts more or less frequently. Most herbs will need to be watered about once a week or when the soil feels dry to the touch. If you live in a climate that is extremely hot or prone to drought, you will want to water the plants twice a week. You should water your herbs in the morning, between six and ten, so that the water does not evaporate in the heat and allow the roots to soak in and absorb the water.

Trimming Your Herbs

Although cutting parts of your herbs seems counterintuitive, trimming them for their health is essential. There are various reasons you might trim your herbs, including harvesting, cutting stems for propagation, or removing dying or dead steps. You must trim your plants because it stops them from growing too out of control. When a plant grows out of control, it becomes harder to maintain and more susceptible to disease, pests, and death as it will need more nutrients.

How to trim your plants:

1. You can trim your plants by pinching off dying leaves or using scissors or clippers, ensuring that your hands or the tools are clean.

2. Cut the stem at the base when trimming to harvest and remove the leaves. Make sure you are harvesting before the flowers of a plant bloom because your herbs will lose some of their flavors when it occurs.
3. When you are harvesting, do it in the morning or afternoon.
4. Some herbs, such as sage, rosemary, and thyme, will become woody in texture as they age. Trimming these areas will help to maintain the health of the plant.

Pruning Your Herbs

Pruning is very similar to trimming as they both deal with cutting plant parts to improve its health. Pruning is the act of cutting the leaves and sometimes parts of the stem to promote more growth. Pruning helps to enhance the development of your plants, and when you prune when your plant is young, it can often help the plant have a better shape and fullness of leaves. After you have harvested your plant, consider pruning to help promote more growth after the harvest.

Leafier plants should be pruned right after harvesting, as the plants tend to die after harvesting when this is not done.

How to prune your plants:

1. Always prune from top to bottom. The leaves on the bottom of your plant are typically more prominent and help keep it sturdy, so you don't

want to remove them.
2. To ensure a bushier plant with more leaves, cut 1-2 inches off the end of your stems. When you cut into the stem, it encourages the plant to grow two separate branches from the spot you cut, allowing for more growth.
3. Make sure your tools are clean. For your indoor herbs, the pinch-off method also works for pruning.

Staking Your Herbs

Depending on the type of herbs you are growing, they can grow tall; when this happens, they need more support. Staking is the process of inserting a stake into the ground or pot or attaching some form of support to your plant, allowing the stems to be protected from breakage, especially when there is a lot of rain or wind.

The single-stake method is best for container plants or tiny gardens. When using the single stake method, you will insert whatever you are using for support in the pot or plant in the garden. You can aid the plant by wrapping any stems around it. You can also use the multiple stake method if you have numerous plants that need extra support.

Common plants that need stakes include peppers, gourds, pumpkins, pole beans, blackberries, cucumbers, melons, tomatoes, and peas.

Here are some tips to consider when staking your plants:

- Always aim for sturdiness. You don't want the stakes to collapse or fall over when staking your plants.
- If your plants need to be staked, do it when planting them. Staking when you are planting is much easier than trying to wrestle a full-grown plant and will give your plant some guidance on where to grow.
- Never staple or zip tie your plants to their stakes. Use twine or string to tie your plant to its stakes.
- Consider the type of plant you have and the type of stake you need. Plants like pole beans do not need big steaks because they are lighter and smaller, while tomatoes will need more support.

After the basics for maintaining your garden, you must also consider what to do when you have unwanted pests and diseases and what to do when winter comes.

Pest Control

Every garden will experience pests at some point in their lives. When these pests decide to make your garden their home and do not leave, that is when you need to step in and practice some pest control. First, we must discuss what the term pest means. A pest in your garden is an insect or animal that is harmful to the health of your plants. Examples of insects in your garden that are not categorized as pests include bees and earthworms. These insects are vital to the health of your outdoor garden and should not be exterminated in the same way you would an infestation.

Pest control is the act of minimizing, managing, removing, or controlling harmful insects and pests from your garden. When dealing with pests in your garden, you should always seek professional help. Professionals will know how to identify the pest you have and can educate you on the impact they would have on your garden, and they will safely remove the pests without harming your herbs. After you have had a professional come to look at your garden, they will treat the problem and develop a plan with you that will help keep pests from taking over your garden again. If you try to practice pest control on your own, you can risk killing your plants.

After consulting a pest control expert, they might tell you to maintain your garden using pesticides. If this is the case, you should always ensure that you safely handle and use pesticides appropriately. When using at-home pesticides, follow these rules:

- Never use outdoor pesticides inside. Outdoor pesticides are designed to remain toxic for longer, keeping pests away. If you use these indoors, you expose yourself and others to these toxins, which is very dangerous.
- Follow the directions on the label. Do not overuse pesticides because they can lead to the death of your plants or kill beneficial insects.
- Always keep your pesticides in the original containers and dispose of them properly. Pesticides can be highly harmful to the environment when not disposed of properly.

Common pests in your garden that cause harm to your plants include spider mites, whiteflies, flea beetles, parsley worms, weevils, spittlebugs, and lead miners.

Common Diseases of an Herb Garden

Your garden contracting a disease is one of the worst things that can happen. Many diseases are not seen until it's too late, and some of your plants are already infected or, worse, your entire garden. There are also cases where you might have bought diseased seeds or plants. You can help prevent the diseases from forming by keeping the plants in an ideal environment, but sometimes diseases will crawl their way into a perfectly healthy garden and ravage the plants you have.

Like humans, plants can fall victim to numerous pathogens,

including white mold, Botrytis blight, powdery mildew, bacterial leaf blights and spots, crown rot and aerial rot, and Pythium root rot (Chase, n.d.). Pathogens such as these can be hazardous to your herb gardens because they affect the plant genus families Lamiaceae and Apiaceae; many of the common herbs we grow are a part of these families. Herbs in these families include cilantro, dill, parsley, basil, lavender, mint, oregano, sage, rosemary, and thyme.

Pathogens are not the only form of disease that can affect your herb garden. There are numerous ways your garden can become infected. Common diseases and their causes include:

- Damping-off diseases can occur at any stage of a plant's life, but your plant is most vulnerable at the sowing stage. This disease can be treated with fungicide during sowing, but this comes with risks of decreasing the speed your seed germinates and the percentage of the seeds that grow.
- Seed-borne diseases are not as common but can affect how plants grow and absorb water. The bacteria Xanthomonas, common in seed-borne diseases, can cause leaf spots which affect how a plant absorbs water. If the leaves stay wet overnight, you can notice a plant has leaf spots.
- Propagating is a great way to help add more plants to your garden but needing to start from scratch, but it comes with an increased chance of bacterial blights. It is like a human getting a cut

when you cut a plant to propagate. It opens the possibility of bacterial infections.
- Too much watering can cause root rot and fungal diseases. Herbs don't typically thrive in highly wet soil, so when their roots are emersed in waterlogged soil, they become more prone to fungal infections and root rot.

It can be hard to recognize your plants' disease until it is too late. Once you notice that your plants might have a disease, try to determine the cause. Testing your soil can help show the presence of any bacteria and pathogens that might harm your plants. This will give you the sign that you need to change your soil.

There are multiple ways to help reduce the risk of diseases in your garden. The first way is to buy healthy plants. Determining if a seed pack is healthy is nearly impossible, but when purchasing seedlings, inspect the plant closely, looking at the undersides of leaves and the steps to ensure there is no sign of infection or spotting. The following way to prevent infection is to ensure you are not overcrowding your garden. Proper space allows for growth and aeration, helping reduce disease risk.

The last way to help prevent diseases in your garden is to take proper care of your plants and maintain them! Following the plant tag or seed packet instructions will help keep your plant at top health and fight any infections. Maintaining your plants through pruning will help remove any stems that are looking sick. Pruning and harvesting your herbs helps to promote further growth and keep the plant healthy.

Natural Fertilizers for Herbs

Fertilizers are needed for maintaining your gardens because, after a while, the soil you are using will start losing the essential nutrients. Fertilizers also help to boost the growth of your plants. Depending on the plant, you will fertilize them differently. Herbs are plants that do not need much fertilizing because they are not heavy feeders. If you are growing herbs in containers, it is recommended that you fertilize them more than you would herbs outside.

You can buy synthetic and natural fertilizers or make your own, which we will discuss briefly. If you plan to purchase fertilizer, make sure you are buying natural. Synthetic fertilizer is only suitable for the short-term health of the plant because rather than feeding the plant and the soil, it removes the nutrients from the soil. Organic or natural fertilizer provides nutrients to both the plant and the soil, keeping them healthy for longer.

You can buy numerous types of fertilizer, including liquid fertilizers or slow-release granules. If you want to give your herbs a boost of nutrients, use liquid fertilizers. Liquid fertilizers are water-soluble and absorbed quickly by the plant and soil. If you are fertilizing this way, you will follow the direction of the container and mix in the appropriate amount of water before pouring it around the base of the plant.

Slow-release granules do just as they say and slowly

release nutrients into the soil for the plant to absorb. If you go for the slow-release option, you do not need to fertilize as often.

The time of the day you fertilize does not matter, but you should never fertilize a drooping plant or appears to be under stress because it has the opposite effect that you want and might even kill your plants.

DIY

You do not need to go out and buy yourself fertilizers; you can make your own. There are numerous kitchen and natural waste items you can use for fertilizers. Everyday items that you can use for fertilizer include:

- Grass clippings are rich in nitrogen, and when you lay about a half-inch on top of the soil, it acts as a mulch and blocks weeds.
- Manure (although not everyone's everyday item) can be used as a fertilizer because it is rich in nitrogen and other essential nutrients.
- Tree leaves help to retain moisture and can attract earthworms. You can crush tree leaves and mix them into potting soil or till (use a machine to break apart the soil) the leaves into the ground.
- Kitchen scraps are great for creating compost, but you can also directly mix them into the soil. Crush eggshells and incorporate them into the soil. You can also use the water from cooking to water your plants as it holds some of the

nutrients from the foods you are cooking. Bananas are another excellent kitchen scrap to use. Wash the peels to remove any traces of pesticides, then bury them and allow them to compost naturally.
- Coffee grounds are great for plants that thrive in slightly acidic soils as it helps to increase acidity levels. Soak six cups of coffee ground for a week, then water your plants with the infused water.

Create the Best Compost

1. As I mentioned with kitchen scraps, composting is another way to fertilize your garden. We touched briefly on compost in an earlier chapter, but here is a more extensive breakdown of how to make your compost. Composting takes time, about two to eight weeks, so be sure that you start composting way before you need to start using it. Follow these steps to make the best compost for your garden:
2. Fill your compost bin with two-thirds carbon and one-third nitrogen materials. To speed up the composting, use smaller pieces of your organic material. Also, do not use branches as they will take longer to compost.
3. When layering your materials spray each layer to keep the pile moist. Keep the moisture level similar to a wrung-out sponge.
4. You can further the composting speed by

buying compost inoculants and mixing them with water.
5. Mix and turn the mix every three days.
6. If you are aiming for a fast compost pile, watch the temperature. A fast pile will reach 120 degrees Fahrenheit by day two, 130 degrees Fahrenheit for a couple of days after, and then will reduce in temperature, around 110 degrees Fahrenheit. Once the temperature is down, the compost might be done.
7. The mix is done when compost is sweet-smelling, dark, and crumbling.

Why You Need to Prepare your Herbs for Winter and How to Do It

Fertilizer and compost are essential for gardening health and are used during the growing season, but maintenance of your garden does not stop after you have harvested your herbs. An outdoor garden needs care throughout the winter, which starts with prepping your garden. Depending on your climate, the winter season might bring on a lot of cold weather and even snow. If you live in this climate, you need to prepare your plants, or they will go through a shock and can die. Preparing your plants will ensure that you have healthy plants ready to grow in spring.

There are multiple steps you need to take to winterize your plants, including:

1. Stop fertilizing your plants in August. When

you fertilize too late in the year, it encourages more growth that will still be delicate come winter and will die.
2. Continue to water plants regularly during the late summer and the fall. Plants under stress due to a lack of water are more susceptible to damage from the cold.
3. Prune your perennials, including mint, thyme, lavender, oregano, tarragon, fennel, and chives. Perennials are very hardy in the winter and require little winterizing.

One big part of winterizing your plants is covering them, like how we cover ourselves with a blanket when we are cold. The time you cover your plants will differ depending on how old the plant is and the hardiness of the plant. Young plants are more susceptible to the cold and need to be covered earlier in the year. The location of your plant also matters because if it is near other structures, such as trees or bushes, it will be more protected and need less coverage. There are numerous things you can use to cover plants, including:

- floating row coverings, which is a polyester cover
- cardboard boxes
- quilts
- black plastic - not clear as it will cause a greenhouse effect

Before covering your plants, add a layer of mulch to help protect them from cold temperatures. Move any outdoor container plants into your garage or house if you can. If you cannot move them indoors, group container plants and cover them.

Take your material of choice and gently lay it on top to cover your plants. Secure the edges of the material with a brick or rocks so it cannot blow away.

Low-Maintenance Herbs

Low-maintenance herbs can be the best options for beginners because they won't take too much of your day, are cost-effective, and can be a great learning experience for anyone trying to grow herbs for the first time. Low-maintenance herbs you can try include:

- Lavender is a herb that people will use for medicinal purposes and fragrances. It is easy to grow indoors and out and can be dried and used in teas. This herb is also great at repelling unwanted pests from your garden.
- Rosemary is one of the most popular herbs and, along with many others on this list, is relatively low maintenance. Rosemary also repels unwanted pests.
- Thyme is a herb that comes in two varieties, edible and for decorative purposes. When buying seeds or seedlings, make sure to purchase the appropriate array. Thyme is an excellent herb for drying and storing for later use.
- Mint is an excellent herb for cooking and medicinal use. Mint, along with many of the

herbs on this list, are plants that can live for years and is extremely easy to propagate. Mint can become invasive in your garden, so plant it in its pot.
- Chives are great for someone who doesn't want to worry too much about sunlight as they prefer to be slightly shaded and require light watering.
- Oregano is a drought-tolerant herb, meaning you do not need to be worried about being on a strict watering schedule. If you miss a few days, the plant isn't going to die.
- Parsley is another common herb that beginners will grow and needs little maintenance to bounce back after harvesting.
- Tarragon is an herb that you can buy in two regional versions. The first is Russian tarragon, which is more bitter but is hardy enough to withstand cold weather, while French tarragon is not as bitter but is not as hardy.
- Fennel needs to be planted out of direct sunlight and forms flowers that will release seeds, allowing the plant to sow new seeds without any work.

High-Maintenance Herbs

After you have some experience with growing herbs, you can start trying to grow more demanding ones. High-maintenance herbs will require more of your time to take care of them. They will be finicky, and you will likely face more challenges. High-maintenance herbs include coriander, dill, sage, and lemongrass.

These herbs are popular, but people find them very hard to keep alive. One of the biggest reasons you might find that these plants are harder to keep alive is that individuals will buy seedlings from a grocery store or supermarket. These plants are likely close to the produce and cooler areas, so their sensitivity makes it harder to recover when brought home and into a warmer climate. Another reason is that people do not dedicate time to care for their plants, and unlike more hardy plants, these are more demanding and need more care.

High-maintenance herbs are more sensitive to their environments, and even if one area is off, they are more likely to die than low-maintenance herbs. Reading seed packets and plant tags and following their specifications will lower the risk of your plants dying.

Starting a garden comes with the responsibility of maintaining it. There are many parts when it comes to maintaining your garden, but now you know all of them, even if you don't need all of them. It is essential to learn the basics of dealing with pests and diseases and winterizing your plants, even if you never have to deal with these aspects of keeping a garden. The point of starting a garden and maintaining it is to harvest the herbs, veggies, or fruits that you grow. In the next chapter, you will learn everything you need to know about harvesting your plants and ensuring they remain healthy afterward.

Fun Fact: Composting inside your greenhouse can help maintain warm temperatures in the winter. If you choose to compost in your greenhouse, ensure proper ventilation

Chapter 5: Harvesting

What is the point of gardening if you can't harvest what you are growing? When we talk about harvesting, you can't just go into your garden and start trimming your plants all willy-nilly. There are specific times of your plant's growth cycle when you should be harvesting different parts of your plant. When we think about herbs, we often think there is only one area you can harvest, but there are multiple parts you can harvest. They must be harvested at the right time so that your plant can continue to grow healthy.

Harvesting Herbs 101

Harvesting seems like a cut-a-dry experience, but there are various things that you must consider when you are harvesting. You must think about the time of year, how often you will harvest, and how to harvest. There will be different methods to use when harvesting depending on the plant. Even amongst herbs, various ways and times are needed to keep the plant healthy and thriving.

Herbs such as basil are leafy annual herbs and should be harvested by pinching the tips of stems and removing the leaves. Herbs such as thyme, oregano, and sage are leafy perennial herbs and should be harvested by cutting the stem and collecting sprigs. Herbs such as lavender, cilantro, and parsley are long-stemmed herbs and should be harvested by cutting close to the branch. It is essential to understand the method and time of harvesting for each of your herbs because if done incorrectly, you can harvest too late or too soon, causing you to lose essential qualities of the plant and leading to the plant's death.

After harvesting, you might notice that you have too much product for yourself. If this is the case, there is no reason to worry. There are multiple ways that you can use an overabundance of harvested material, including:

- giving them to others or selling them to make a small income
- dry herbs and use them later
- freeze herbs to use later

Even after these methods, if you have some leftovers, do not throw them in the garbage. Instead, compost them and use them to feed other plants.

Depending on the plant, you might be able to use your hands to harvest, especially when it comes to small herbs that you keep in your home. Additional tools you might need to harvest your herbs include scissors or kitchen shears, fruit harvester, leaf or thorn stripper, herb stripper, and harvest basket. You do not need to go and buy these tools to harvest your plants, but they help speed up the process and make it easier.

Why Is It Important to Harvest Herbs at the Right Time

The timing of harvesting is crucial to the plant's health and how tasty the herb is going to taste. When you harvest too soon or too late, it can alter the taste of the herb. The harvest time is critical if you plan to dry or freeze your herbs because you want the highest level and essential oils.

Essential oils fluctuate in potency throughout the year, and for the most flavor, you want to harvest when these essential oils are at an all-time high. Depending on the plant, the time of year and the frequency of the plant having high levels of essential oils will differ.

Herbs such as oregano and basil should be harvested before the plant's flower. Once these herbs start to flower, the flavor is impacted. If you are growing herbs inside, you can harvest them whenever you want just to have access to fresh herbs throughout the season. There will always be flavor in harvesting herbs, but the strength of the flavor will differ throughout the season; however if you are growing herbs to freeze or dry them, harvest them at peak time. I will discuss the times to harvest different plants later in this chapter.

Tips to Harvest Herbs

Harvesting your herbs can seem tricky because of all the different variables you must consider, but don't worry. Throughout this chapter, I will walk you through everything you need to know about harvesting, first with these tips:

- Promote further growth while also harvesting leaves by cutting a sprig and removing the leaves.
- Remove the buds of the plant before they flower so the taste is not affected.
- You should always pick your herbs very close to the time you will use them so that you do not lose the aromatic nature of the herbs.
- If your plant becomes leggy or very thin in growth, cut and harvest the plant to promote fuller growth.
- Water the day before you plan to harvest. A stressed-out plant tastes different; thus, you want it to be the least stressed possible.
- Frequent harvests are good as they reduce flowering and promote more growth.

- Certain herbs need to be at the right height. Herbs such as basil need to be about six to eight inches high.
- When cutting sprigs off, cut at a node (a protrusion that signifies another branch is going to grow there)

Most Common Herb Gardening Mistakes

Everyone makes mistakes, especially in the beginning while we are still learning. Here I will tell you the most common mistakes people make while gardening herbs to help you avoid them. The most common herb gardening mistakes are:

- You are not growing your plants in the right spot. We discussed this in the earlier chapter but finding the right place for your plants will ensure they have the perfect environment for growth.
- You are not trimming and pruning your herbs regularly. Trimming and pruning your plants, as discussed in the last chapter, is essential to maintaining your plants and helps promote more growth. Your plant can have stunted growth when you don't do this regularly.
- You are overcrowding your herbs. When you group your plants too closely, it will cause them to be unable to spread out as much as they need and cause nutrient deficiencies and stunted growth.
- You are allowing the flowers on your herbs to

seed. For some herbs, such as basil, allowing the plant's flowers to bloom and seed before harvesting causes the flavor to be reduced.
- You are not watering your herbs enough. All plants need water, so you must ensure you water them enough, or they will wilt and die. Watering your herbs ensures they will be strong and produce more yield.
- Planting mint and other unfriendly herbs directly in your garden, not in their pots. Mint is one of the worst plants you can grow alongside others, so make sure to plant it in its pot, even if your garden is outdoors.
- You forget to mulch your herb garden. Mulch is essential for your garden as it helps to keep weeds away and, during the winter, helps keep the roots secure and warm.
- You are not giving your plants the fertilizer they need. Not fertilizing your plants drains the soil of essential nutrients faster and causes your plants to grow weaker. Your plants occasionally need an extra nutrition boost, and fertilizer is how you do this.
- You are not inspecting seedlings when you buy them. If you are buying seedlings, you need to inspect them as much as possible to ensure that you are not purchasing a diseased or pest-infested plant. If you don't inspect your plants, you might introduce disease and pests into your garden, which can be detrimental to the plant's

health.
- You are not adding proper drainage to your pots or soil. Drainage is essential for the plant's health as it stops the roots from being submerged in water and rotting.

When Should You Harvest?

Understanding when to harvest your plants, depending on the purpose of the plants, is vital to getting the most benefits from the plant. Depending on the herb, there are multiple parts that you can harvest, including the leaves, flowers, and roots. This section will learn when the best time of day to harvest is and when you need to harvest your leaves, flowers, and roots. Lastly, we will talk about harvesting according to the moon cycle.

What Time is Best to Harvest Herbs

Although it doesn't seem like it would matter, there are times of the day when it is better to harvest your plants. As we discussed, herbs with flowers should be harvested before they flower. Frequent harvesting and removal of flower buds will allow you to harvest the plant for longer without the change in flavor that happens once an herb flowers. When harvesting, try to aim for the morning, especially if you grow your herbs outdoors. Aim to harvest your herbs after the dew has dried but before the sun is beating down and hot. When the leaves of your herbs are tender, they are ready for harvesting.

Tip: Do not wash the leaves of your herbs unless you have used pesticides or other chemicals, as aromatic oils will be lost and will not be as fragrant or flavorful when cooking and eating.

Flowering herbs such as chamomile and lavender should be harvested before their flowers bloom. Herbs such as dill, coriander, and fennel that are grown for their seeds should be harvested when the seed pods start to change color.

When to Harvest Leaves

Herbs harvested for their leaves are best picked before flowering. If you harvest frequently and cut flower blooms, you can harvest leaves the entire growing season. The taste of herbs after they have flowered can become bitter. If you are growing herbs indoors, you are likely using them regularly; if this is the case harvesting your herbs doesn't need to fall under a specific time of the year. Even if your garden is indoors, you should harvest your leaves in the morning because the plant's energy is mainly in the leaves in the morning, and as the day goes by, the energy will move to the flowers if the herb has them.

Annual herbs are some of the best for harvesting leaves, especially throughout the entire season, because you can prune up to 50-75% of the plant, and it will still recover. Be mindful of how much you are harvesting from a plant because taking too much away from it can cause it to enter into a state of shock and die.

When to Harvest Flowers

Harvesting herbs does not only mean harvesting the leaves. With any plant, multiple parts can be harvested, and many uses for the different parts. If your herbs have flowers that can be used or are a flowering herb, such as lavender and chamomile, harvest them between noon and two in the afternoon. If you want to use the flowers of a herb, but don't want the bitter taste that might be associated with the change, consider harvesting in the early growing season and then harvesting the flowers later in the year. As we said in the last section, the plant's energy moves throughout the day, which is held mainly in the flowers at this time. If you are harvesting the herb's flowers, ensure it is also a sunny day, as the flowers will have more energy.

When to Harvest Roots

We don't often think about plant roots being something we harvest, but we can. Roots cannot be harvested at all times of the year. Harvest roots in the winter, early spring, or late fall when the plant is prepared for winter and is almost in a sleep state. Between late spring and early fall, the plant focuses on growing new leaves and flowers, so you want to ensure you are not harvesting roots at this time.

Roots will have the most energy in the afternoon and night, allowing them to have the most energy and herbal properties possible.

Use a garden fork to loosen the soil, and dig up some roots to harvest. Use a spade or shears to cut roots off the root crown. After cutting the roots, gently bang them on the ground to loosen any soil. After removing most of the dirt, you must wash the roots before using them. Unlike the flowers and leaves you can harvest and use a few days later, you should immediately dry or freeze your roots.

Harvesting Herbs According to the Moon Cycle

This method of harvesting is less popular than looking at the plant's growth, but it is not entirely disregarded. According to the moon cycles, theories around harvesting come from the idea that the ground's vitality and richness are more prominent during the waxing and waning moons. According to theories of harvesting according to the moon cycle, you should be harvesting while the moon is waning for root harvesting.

If you plan to harvest using moon cycles, the waning and waxing moons are the most popular times as the plants have had time to soak up energy from the previous moon cycles or the full moon from that month's moon cycle. Part of this harvesting also comes with the instinct to think a plant is full of life and ready to be harvested.

Typically, beginners will not use this method of harvesting as they haven't had the time to grow the instincts or confidence to tell when a plant is ready to be harvested.

Harvesting is the last step before preparing your herbs for use. Depending on the herb, there are multiple different uses that you can get out of it. Before diving deeper into the numerous ways you can prepare herbs and get all the medicinal benefits from them, we have to explore the different kinds of medicinal herbs you can grow, their advantages, and the medicinal uses you can get from them.

Fun Fact: Drying herbs increase their flavor, meaning that you should only use about a third of the amount of dried herbs you would use of fresh herbs.

Chapter 6: Medicinal Herbs to Grow

One of the biggest reasons you might be starting a garden is to get the health and medicinal benefits from the growing herbs. Everyone at some point in their lives becomes ill; the reasons why we become sick are entirely personal. You might be more predisposed to certain illnesses, or your mental health has been on the decline, and your physical health is starting to take a hit as well. Anyone that has needed to get medication from a doctor will know they are costly. Depending on the illness or disease you are battling, you can spend thousands of dollars on medication.

Starting a herb garden can help reduce costs as it can help improve your health to the point where you don't need the prescription anymore or need it less frequently. However, some diseases and illnesses need medication to help manage them, so it is not a 100% guarantee that your medical issues will be erased by introducing medicinal herbs into your life. I want to clarify that medicinal herbs do not work for everyone. Some people are more susceptible to the medicinal benefits of plants than others. There is also the possibility that your illness or disease might be so severe that even through medicinal herbs, you still need the help of prescriptions to manage your health.

Before starting a garden, you want to be sure that the plants you are growing will give you the benefits you want. This chapter will focus on what medicinal herbs are, their history, testimonials from people about the healing properties of herbs, and 20 medicinal herbs for you to try growing.

What Are Medicinal Herbs?

Before looking at the definition of medicinal herbs, we should look at what a herb is. Derived from the Latin word *herba*, it "refers to any part of the plant like fruit, seed, stem, bark, flower, leaf, stigma or a root, as well as a non-woody plant" (National Health Portal India, 2017). Medicinal herbs are any plant or part of a plant used for medicinal purposes. Depending on the plant, its medicinal use for it will differ.

Medicinal herbs have been around long before humanity was, yet why are they not used widely worldwide. As society moved into modernity, traditional medicine, such as medicinal herbs, took a back seat, especially in the West, as technology and scientific advancements were made. The use of medicinal plants declined in the West, but as Western ideologies change and people look to natural remedies and Eastern medicine, it has been on the rise once again. Before we look at the types of herbs you can grow in your backyard, let's dive into the past and look at the history of medicinal herbs.

History of Medicinal Herbs

Humanity's history with medical herbs goes back to when humans gained consciousness and started experimenting with herbs. The information we learned from ancient cultures and how they practiced medicine shaped our medical advancements today. In ancient civilizations such as Greece, doctors would study animals to see what plants they would eat, especially if they looked ill. Doctors in ancient cultures did not have the same technology or information today, so they had to experiment with herbs and how they worked concerning treating someone's ailments. Western medicine was shaped by Greek medicine, one of the most significant examples being the Hippocratic oath that doctors still take today. The Greeks and Romans also had gods to reign over medical practices. Medical sanctums were created to treat patients, and priests and priestesses of gods and goddesses of medicine would come to pray for god and help with the healing process.

However, the history of medicinal herbs encompasses the Greeks and their medical advancements. We must look at various cultures, including Native Americans, Chinese, and Ayurveda.

Native American

The medicinal herbs available to the Greeks differ entirely from those available in North America. Although nowadays we might be able to grow them here, even just a hundred or so years ago, that wasn't the case. An excellent source for learning about medicinal herbs available in

North America and their purposes is to look towards Native American culture and their teachings.

Before white settlers made their way onto North American soil, the Native Americans had already discovered the medicinal properties of many of the native plants, including goldenseal, yerba santa, echinacea, and blue cohosh. This knowledge was vital when white settlers arrived as there were no antibiotics or other medicine. Luckily, the Native Americans shared this information with pioneers allowing it to be integrated into the medicinal practices they had already established. When settlers first arrived, they relied heavily on the Native Americans to help them to develop their society. Doctors in the early settlements would heavily depend on the information of the Native Americans to treat a variety of health issues, including constipation, snakebites, and burns.

Specific examples of medicinal plants and their medicinal use include:

- Roots of red trillium were used as a pain reliever during childbirth.
- Witch hazel was used to soothe sore muscles.
- A salve made from balsamroot was used to help heal flesh wounds.

These are only a few examples of the medicinal practices and information the Native Americans shared with settlers that were fundamental to their survival and prosperity.

Years after white settlers had arrived, they were still depending on the wealth of knowledge the Native Americans had provided them with as the Civil War started to develop. Doctors had to treat many wounded soldiers, and without the knowledge the Native Americans had shared with them, it wouldn't be possible. Medicinal herbs such as partridgeberry, sassafras, tulip trees, dogwood, and the bark and leaves of white oaks were used heavily throughout the Civil War as they helped to:

- prevent infection
- promote blood clotting to stop someone from bleeding out
- lower fever
- relieve pain

Diseases such as scurvy would run through settling camps, especially during the Gold Rush. Native Americans in the area showed them that *Claytonia Perfoliata*, a plant native to the Sierra Nevada area, would heal their symptoms.

The Native American's knowledge and wisdom of medicinal plants were vital to the success of North American settlers, yet as we look back at history, it is often ignored. This is because settlers already knew medicinal herbs local to Europe, and they combined this information with that of the Natives. When these two herbal traditions combined, the importance of the Native Americans and their knowledge was forgotten.

Chinese

Eastern medicine has been rising in popularity throughout Western culture in recent years. Traditional Chinese medicine (TCM) focuses on restoring and maintaining the yin-yang balance to heal diseases and prevent them from occurring. TCM uses various methods to obtain yin-yang balance; one is herbal medicine. The earliest known document of herbal medicine in China is dated around the third century BCE. Yin and yang are two forces within everyone, with yin passive and yang active. Without a balance of passive and active forces, we become more prone to illnesses and diseases.

Herbal therapy in TCM is used to help strengthen our organ function and support the good health associated with establishing a balance between yin and yang energy. Herbal medicines are only one aspect of TCM as people will also use acupuncture, moxa treatment, and cupping alongside herbal medicines. TCM practitioners will focus both on the chemical properties of the herbs but also their essence or signature energy vibration. When someone sees a TCM practitioner, their treatment will be chosen based on their physical ailments and essence.

Historically, western civilizations have brushed aside Eastern medicinal practices as inadequate or fake. However, studies have shown that principles of TCM, such as yin and yang, have scientific backing. Studies demonstrated that TCM's yin and yang principles can be applied to genetic diseases (The Editors of Encyclopedia Britannica, 2019a). Genetic diseases become active when one gene in our genetic sequence is activated; let's say this is the passive or the yin. Because of the natural law, another gene in our genetic sequence is meant to fix the activation of the genetic disease; let's say this is the active or yang. This theory implies that there is a gene that triggers the disease and another that is meant to heal it, and when we identify the healing gene and activate it, it can bring balance back to the body.

Chinese medicine has a vast history but can be broken down into four distinct periods. Between the 29th-27th centuries, BCE was the first period where medicinal practices started to change and grow. The second period occurred in the first half of the fifth century BCE and was primarily led by the career of Bian Qiao. The third period occurred between 150 and 300 CE and is renowned for being a period of great practitioners. The fourth period lasted 1300 years and focused on recording medicinal practices done the years before.

The second half of the 16th century marked a huge change in Eastern Medicine as practitioners started to talk with Western representations and adopted some of their practices.

Ayurveda

Ayurveda, also known as Ayurvedic medicine, are traditional Indian medicinal practice. This form of medicine is prevalent throughout Asia and is characterized by being both curative and preventative. These practices are prevalent in the east, with most of India using them, either exclusively or combined with Western traditions. Ayurveda was initially an oral tradition, much like Native American medicinal practices. An early version of it was written about 5000 years ago in Sanskrit in sacred texts known as the Vedas: The Rig Veda (which was written around 3000-2500 BCE), Sam Veda, Yajur Veda, and Atharva Veda (which was written around 1200-1000 BCE).

These texts were sacred as they were full of magical treatments for several ailments, including fever, diarrhea, cough, abscesses, tumors, seizures, and diseases such as leprosy. These texts also wrote about charms to help with expelling curses. The writing in these texts was adopted into an early form of Ayurveda that is practiced today, except rather than magical treatments, they focused on medicinal treatments.

Much like in Greek history, the medicinal practices of Ayurveda are attributed to a god. In Hindu mythology, the god Brahma is said to have given Dhanvantari, the physician to the gods, the practices of Ayurveda. Between 800 BCE and 1000 CE, medical texts such as Caraka-Samhita and Susruta-Samhita were created by physician

Caraka and surgeon Susruta.

Ayurveda focuses on prevention by emphasizing "the need for a strict code of personal and social hygiene, the details of which depend upon individual, climatic, and environmental needs" (The Editors of Encyclopedia Britannica, 2019b). Common remedies in Ayurveda involve lifestyle changes such as increasing the amount of exercise you do, herbal medicines, and some form of yoga or meditation.

Along with preventative practices, Ayurveda emphasizes curative methods such as herbal medicines, diet, physiotherapy, and external preparations. Ayurveda is a medicinal practice that emphasizes that all aspects of our lives impact our health. It is very similar to the theories around how mental, emotional, and physical health are all interlinked that Western medicine speaks of in the modern-day.

Ayurveda embodies the idea of the body being broken down into the elements: water, earth, air, fire, and ether. There are also theories of the three bodily humors: pitta, vata, and kapha.

10 Easy to Grow Herbs and Their Properties

When starting to grow herbs, picking the easiest ones will reduce some of the initial fear or stress you might have towards starting your herb garden. Here are 10 of the easiest herbs to grow and all the benefits and medical uses you can get out of them.

Basil

Basil is one of the most popular herbs grown because of its easiness and is also a very popular herb for cooking. Basil is most used in Mediterranean dishes, such as adding to pasta sauce. Basil needs about 6 hours of sun and prefers to stay moist. You should water your basil plants about once or twice during hot weeks. Basil plants want about an inch of water each week. You can grow several types of basil plants, including sweet basil, bush basil, Thai basil, cinnamon basil, and lettuce basil.

The benefits you can get from basil differ slightly depending on the type of basil you grow. Sweet basil is the most common basil grown and has the most benefits, including:

- preventing breast, pancreas, and colon cancer
- acting like aspirin as it helps to thin the blood and relax blood vessels
- lowering blood pressure
- reducing memory loss and depression associated with experiencing chronic stress
- supporting recovery for stroke patients and reducing stroke damage
- protecting the stomach from ulcers caused by aspirins
- improving mental processes and alertness
- improving food safety when integrated into food packaging

- reducing bacteria growth that can cause tooth decay
- being used as an alternative for antibiotics
- repelling mosquitos and ticks

There are multiple medicinal uses for basil, including brewing it into a tea to help settle your stomach and soothing your headaches, sore throats, and congestion. Chewing fresh basil leaves can help relieve migraines, and crushing them and applying them to a bug bite can stop itchiness and remove poisons. Basil essential oil can be used to improve mood and concentration.

Mint

Mint is also an easy herb to plant, with multiple types that can fit any minty need that you might need. Mint can be used in drinks and salads. Herbs enjoy part or full sun, depending on the species. Mint likes to grow in moist conditions and should receive about one to two inches of water a week or more during hot weeks.

Mint is so famous not only for its taste but also for the multiple benefits you can get. Benefits of mint include:

- rich in nutrients such as fiber, vitamin A, iron, manganese, and folate
- can relieve symptoms of irritable bowel syndrome and colds
- can relieve indigestion
- can decrease pain associated with breastfeeding
- can see an improvement in brain function

- can help to hide bad breath
- can improve the health and appearance of the skin
- helps alleviate menstrual symptoms

Mint can be used in various ways medicinally. Mint oil can be used on the skin to reduce inflammation, pain, and itchiness associated with pimples, rashes, bug bites, and sunburns. You can make mint teas to help relieve cold and sinus symptoms or chew on fresh mint leaves.

Chives

Chives are very popular as garnishes and have a flavor similar to onions. The flowers of chives are also edible. Chives can grow in part and under full sun. Soil drainage is vital for growing chives as they should be watered frequently.

Chives, specifically garlic chives, are rich in essential vitamins and nutrients such as Vitamin C, Vitamin A, potassium, riboflavin, iron, beta carotene, and thiamin.

Vitamin C is essential for fighting symptoms of the common cold and fever. The other vitamins and nutrients are vital in maintaining blood pressure, keeping your blood count, and improving immunity.

The medical uses of chives include:

- Steeping chives and using the water to reduce inflammation.
- They are full of antioxidants and, when eaten regularly, can improve skin and hair health.
- Raw chives are antibacterial and fight against Ecoli, staphylococcus, and salmonella.
- Regular conception can reduce the likelihood of developing colorectal and stomach cancers.
- Use chive extract on hair to increase blood flow to the scalp and treat scalp infections. It can also be used to wash other wounds on the body.

Parsley

Parsley is popular because of its versatility and can be used in nearly any dish. Parsley should be grown in partly shaded areas, leaning on more sun than shade, and needs moist soil. You should water your parsley twice a week with about two inches each time.

Parsley has multiple benefits, including:

- contains various nutrients such as vitamins A, C, K, folate, and potassium
- has numerous antioxidants such as vitamin C, flavonoids, and carotenoids

- great for bone health because it is full of vitamin K and potassium
- fighting cancer
- protecting eye health
- might improve heart health
- parsley extract is antibacterial
- improves digestive and urinary tract health

You can make sauces such as pesto and salads to increase the vitamins and nutrients you are getting into your diet. Parsley can also be made into an infusion to help boost urinary tract health. These infusions can help fight and reduce urinary tract infections, edema, kidney stones, and cystitis.

Rosemary

Rosemary is an evergreen, woody shrub that is incredibly hardy. These plants enjoy the full sun but prefer light watering. You should water rosemary once a week during the summer and once every two weeks during other seasons. During hot weeks, do not double up on the watering; just water it a little more than usual.

Rosemary is another herb that has numerous benefits, including:

- boosts your immune system and improves blood circulation
- improves mental processes, including memory and focus
- can help prevent baldness and promote hair

growth, reduce the speed of greying, and treats dry scalp and dandruff
- improves digestive issues, including loss of appetite, gas, and heartburn
- can help fight bacterial infections
- helps protect skin from sun damage
- enhances mood, relieves stress, and clears the mind

You can use rosemary for its medicinal properties in many different ways. You can use rosemary essential oil to improve mood, stress, and mental processes. You can also make tea from rosemary and get some health benefits or use it in your hair. Eating rosemary will give you all the physical health benefits you need, whether fresh or dry.

Oregano

Oregano is the perfect herb for a combination of sweetness and spice. Everyday items you can pair with oregano include lamb, tomatoes, and eggplants. Oregano needs full sun and likes to be drier. When the soil is dried, you should water it, but not too much.

The benefits of consuming oregano include:

- an influx of antioxidants
- an increase of antibacterial compounds
- helps fight cancer
- can help reduce the symptoms of viral infections such as diarrhea, stomach pain, and nausea
- decreases inflammation

The oil of oregano has been shown to have numerous medicinal uses. This oil is extracted from the leaves and has been shown to have many uses, including as a pain reliever, a fungicide, an anti-inflammatory, and a topical treatment for bug bites. Dried oregano leaves also have medicinal uses, such as being turned into a paste to help with itching, pain, swelling, sores, and aching muscles. Dried leaves can be chopped or turned into a paste and added to gelatin for a homemade health booster. Adding dried oregano leaves to a bath can help soothe muscles, aching feet, and joints. Lastly, you can also make tea from fresh or dried oregano leaves.

Thyme

Thyme is an herb often added to meat dishes, especially chicken. Thyme likes to be in full sun and should only be watered once it has dried.

Thyme is truly timeless regarding the benefits and medicinal uses you can get out of it. When thyme is a regular part of your diet, you will see multiple benefits, including:

- reduction in anxiety
- improve skin health
- relief from respiratory issues such as cough and bronchitis
- antibacterial
- relieves pain, specifically menstrual cramps, as it is an analgesic and antispasmodic
- used as a remedy for oral thrush

Use thyme in your meals, including making teas, to get the physical health benefits. Thyme essential oil can be used to help reduce anxiety and help with your cough.

Dill

Dill is an excellent herb to add to butter, dips, and oils. It can grow up to a meter tall but can be maintained from frequent harvesting. Dill needs full sun and moist soil, especially when growing seeds. Dill needs about 1-2 inches of water each week.

Dill is a delicious herb, but it comes with a vast amount of benefits, including:

- helping to regulate diabetes
- helping to prevent infections
- improving bone health
- relieving symptoms of insomnia
- promotes digestive health

There are multiple medicinal uses that you can get out of dull, including adding it to dishes such as salads, soups, and garnish. Dill is typically not made into tea, but you could make a dill infusion shot to boost vitamins and nutrients.

Sage

Sage is commonly used in meat dishes involving pork and in soups and stuffings. Sage needs full sun and should be watered very lightly about one to two times a week.

Sage has some of the most amounts of benefits you can get from a single herb, including:

- being packed with nutrients such as vitamin K, iron, manganese, calcium, and antioxidants
- has antimicrobial effects that can support oral health
- can reduce the effects of menopausal symptoms
- lower bad cholesterol and blood sugar levels
- improves brain health and memory
- helps to protect from cancer
- improves bone health
- combats aging
- alleviate diarrhea

Along with being loaded with benefits, you can get multiple medicinal uses from sage. Make sage oxymel and consume it to relieve colds, coughs, fevers, and indigestion. Teas can also be made. Create a steam bath from a hot bowl of water and some sage to help with congestion.

Coriander

Coriander is a citrusy herb that is better grown during cooler months. These herbs need good drainage and can be grown in part or full sun. Coriander needs about one inch of water each week.

There are numerous benefits to consuming coriander, including:

- lowering blood sugar
- being packed with antioxidants that help to boost immune systems
- can improve heart health
- can protect brain health
- promotes gut and digestion health
- helps to fight infections

- can protect skin health

Coriander has multiple medicinal uses, including using the leaves to create juice and coriander seeds to create spices. Coriander leaf juice has various skin benefits, including helping with acne, oiliness, dryness, and pigmentation. Coriander leaves can also support bone health and maintain eye and vision health. Coriander seeds are just as useful as their leaves as they can lower and regulate blood sugar and digestion. Coriander extract can also help with symptoms of digestive disorders such as ulcerative colitis and increase your libido.

10 Not-as-Easy Herbs to Grow and Their Properties

After you have experience growing some easy herbs, you can start exploring more challenging plants to grow and gain more medicinal benefits.

Lavender

Lavender is a herb that people either love or hate. Lavender is an excellent choice of herb because it can grow in a wide range of soil, even poor quality soil, as long as it has full sun and good drainage. How much you water your lavender will change throughout its life. The lavender you have just planted will need to be watered once or twice a week until the plant is established. When the plant matures, water once every two to three weeks. Once buds start to form, you will begin to water once or twice a week again.

Lavender has many health benefits, including:

- improves sleep
- helps to reduce skin inflammation
- can be used as a pain reliever
- reduces heart rate and lowers blood pressure
- reduces menopausal symptoms, specifically hot flashes
- can help to relieve asthma symptoms
- promotes hair growth
- fights fungal growth
- help to reduce stress

Lavender is an incredibly versatile herb when it comes to its medical uses. You can use lavender oil, the plant, tea, and supplements for various medical uses. Aromatherapy is one of the most common uses of lavender. Using lavender essential oil in a diffuser or diluting it with water as a spray is very common in helping to optimize your bedroom and improve sleep. Lavender oil or creams can also be applied topically to burns or mixed with peppermint to help with headaches.

Dandelion

Dandelion is a plant that people think of as a weed, but it is a herb that has many benefits from consumption. You might notice that you have a specific spot in your yard where dandelions grow, and these will be areas with the full sun they need. Dandelions need a lot of water to grow. Poke your fingers into the soil every two to three days and feel dry water. If it is still moist, wait another day and check again.

Dandelions are brushed aside as weeds, but they have many health benefits, including:

- being packed with nutrients such as vitamins A, C, E, K, and folate
- are rich in the antioxidant beta carotene
- reduces inflammation
- can help to lower and regulate blood sugar levels
- can reduce triglyceride and cholestrol levels
- lowers blood pressure
- boosts liver health
- can help with weight loss
- has cancer-fighting effects
- can help treat constipation and promote digestive health
- can boost your immune system
- helps to prevent skin damage
- helps to boost bone health

Traditional uses of dandelions include being used as a laxative or diuretic. Dandelion leaves help to improve digestion, and the roots help boost kidney, liver, and gallbladder health. Roots and leaves can also help with lowering blood pressure. Dandelion salads are some of the most common ways people consume dandelions.

Yarrow

Yarrow is a herb that has been used in natural medicine for centuries. It needs full sun and needs to be watered very little, about an ounce of water a month.

Yarrow has multiple health benefits, including:

- helps to reduce inflammation
- helps to speed up the healing process
- can help to reduce symptoms of irritable bowel syndrome
- reduces anxiety
- regulates blood sugar
- help to protect the gallbladder and liver
- can boost and support the immune system

Medical uses of yarrow include creating teas from the leaves and flowers, making an infused oil, and creating a tincture. Drinking the tea can improve liver and gallbladder health, lower blood sugar, and help with irritable bowel syndrome. The infused oil can be used to speed up the healing process or used in a diffuser, or dabbed onto the skin to help reduce anxiety. The tincture can be used as an insect repellent.

Stinging Nettle

A plant called the stinging nettle might seem like one that won't have much medicinal use, but it does. To grow stinging nettle, you will need to have full sun and give it about 1-2 inches per week.

Stinging nettle has been used for centuries for its health benefits, such as a pain reliever for muscles, gout, arthritis, eczema, joints, and anemia. It has also been used to treat urinary problems and enlarged prostates in the modern day.

Stinging nettle can be used in a variety of ways for medicinal use. You can dry or freeze the leaves to make teas or create tinctures, creams, or capsules. Leaves, roots, and stems can also be added to soups, smoothies, stews, and stir-frys. If you have any joint or muscle pain, creams made with stinging nettle will be the best way to use this herb medically.

Calendula

Calendula is a herb native to Asia and southern Europe and needs full sun. During the summer, you will want to be consistent with watering and one to one and a half inches of water.

The health benefits of calendula include:

- help to prevent and treat infections
- help to heal external wounds
- ease muscle fatigue
- reduce the likelihood of developing heart disease
- rich in antioxidants

Calendula's most considerable medicinal use is treating external issues such as rashes, minor wounds, infections, and inflammation. The chemicals in calendula flowers help speed up new tissue growth and decrease swelling. Calendula is commonly used for external use and is commonly made into an infused oil or cream. However, it can be made into tea as well. Combining the use of an oil or cream with tea can help to boost your body's natural healing processes and allow you to heal faster.

Chamomile

Chamomile is a very popular herb that is used for tea. Many people will drink chamomile tea and not realize all the benefits they will get from them. Chamomile needs full sun and one to two inches of water per week.

Chamomile has so many benefits, including:

- helps to reduce menstrual cramp pain
- helps to prevent and slow osteoporosis
- lowers blood sugar and can help treat diabetes
- reduces inflammation
- improves relaxation and sleep
- targets cancer cells and helps to prevent cancer

- helps to treat cold symptoms
- can be used to treat eczema

Chamomile tea is only one of the uses you can get from your chamomile plants. Chamomile tea can be used for anyone of any age and has been shown to help with upset stomachs, nausea, heartburn, and vomiting. Chamomile has been shown to help with colicky babies as well.

Fennel

Fennel is one of the only vegetables we will discuss on this list. Many of the other plants that we have talked about are what we can call spices or flowers. Fennel needs full sun and about one inch of water per week.

The health benefits of consuming fennel regularly include:

- helps maintain heart health
- helps to reduce inflammation
- supports healthier skin
- can improve symptoms of anemia
- can help with weight management

The medicinal uses of fennel come primarily from its seeds and oil. Fennel can help with gas, heartburn, bloating, colic, and loss of appetite. Specifically, women have used fennel to help with breast milk production, improve sex drive, regulate menstruation, and make the birthing process easier. Fennel powder has also been used on snakebites as a poultice.

Bay

Bay is a herb that will start in a pot but eventually grow into a tree. Your Bay plant will need to be in full sun, and while it is still in a pot, it will need to be watered regularly. Once your bay plant has become a tree, watering will only be necessary if you have a dry season. If you are experiencing a drought, water the tree every two weeks.

The health benefits of bay include:

- helps to regulate blood sugar levels
- help reduce bacterial infections
- can slow the growth of cancers such as breast and colorectal
- boosts brain functions

Although it is not one of the most common herbs, bay can have a lot of medicinal uses. Creating a paste, infused oil, or tea and treating a wound can help heal, specifically fighting bacteria and infections. Drinking tea made with bay leaves can also help to prevent kidney stones. Bay tea can help improve memory formation and cognition.

Stevia

Stevia is a plant mainly known for making a natural sweetener from its leaves. To grow your stevia, you will need full sun and will have to keep the soil evenly moist.

The health benefits associated with stevia include:

- a great alternative to sugar for those with diabetes as it doesn't contribute to insulin and

blood glucose responses
- can aid with weight loss
- high in antioxidants that help fight pancreatic cancer
- helps to decrease blood sugar

The medical uses of stevia are centered around introducing more healthy foods into your diet that are low in artificial sweeteners and trans fats. Reducing the number of artificial sweeteners and processed foods and learning to use stevia instead of sugar can give you many health benefits.

Lemongrass

Lemongrass is an herb that is used for its leaves and oils. To grow lemongrass, you will want a minimum of 6 hours of sun but aim for full sun. You should also water your lemongrass every few days.

The health benefits of lemongrass include:

- rich in antioxidants
- is antifungal and antibacterial
- reduces inflammation
- helps to lower cholesterol and prevent the development of heart disease
- can help to relieve muscle pain

Medicinally, lemongrass is commonly applied directly to the skin, used through aromatherapy, or taken orally. Aromatherapy will be the least effective, but it can help you to relax and ease muscle tension. Lemongrass leaves and oils can be added to oils or creams and applied topically to fight infections or ease muscle pain. Tea can also be made from lemongrass leaves and used as a mouthwash to fight oral infections or consumed to help reduce cholesterol.

Cooking is one of the easiest ways to introduce medicinal herbs into your diet. The best part of integrating herbs through cooking is that you do not need to learn all sorts of new recipes. Instead, these herbs can be combined into the recipes you already know to help elevate them while also giving you the health benefits associated with them. The most common herbs that are grown for cooking include:

- basil: great for adding to pasta dishes or sauces
- bay: add flavor to a meal with dried leaves, but remove before serving
- rosemary: great for savory dishes such as steak
- chives: pair perfectly with garlic and give an oniony flavor.
- parsley: used as a garnish and also sprinkled in pasta dishes
- thyme: used as a seasoning in savory dishes
- mint: most popularly used in teas or can be added to fruit salads

When growing herbs, there are two categories they can be broken into. The first is perennial herbs, and the second is annual herbs. Whichever type of herb you grow will determine how often you need to plant your herbs.

Perennial Herbs

Perennial herbs are herbs you will not need to replant in the summer. These herbs are easy to grow and are hardy enough to make it through the winter. It might seem like they disappear come winter, but you will notice that they will start to pop up again in the springtime. Some herbs might die throughout the winter, but most will come back in the spring.

Perennial herbs include creeping thyme, oregano, lovage, lemon verbena, lemon balm, parsley, sweet marjoram, sage, fennel, roman chamomile, mint, lavender, salad burnet, chives, sorrel, garlic chives, rosemary, viola, winter savory.

Annual Herbs

Annual herbs have a one-year life cycle and need to be planted yearly if you want to keep growing them. For annual herbs, you will plant their seed in the spring or buy a seedling and plant it, and it will flower and then die in the winter. If you want to postpone the flowering of your herbs, harvest them frequently.

Annual herbs include basil, dill, marjoram, chamomile, fennel, summer savory, coriander/cilantro, and chervil.

You now have all the information you need to start growing the medicinal herbs you need to treat any illness you might be experiencing. Depending on the severity of your symptoms, you might be able to stop spending thousands of dollars on medication and doctors. After you have grown your herbs, you need to learn how to prepare them. Continue reading to find out all the ways you can prepare your herbs.

Fun Fact: Using herbs to flavor and spice your dishes allows you to use less salt and still have a delicious meal. Use oregano, basil, dill, chives, or other herbs to spruce up your meals.

Chapter 7: Preparations

When you think about growing herbs and using them, the first thing that might come to mind is cooking. But even a couple of plants can produce too much for a single person or family to consume only through meals. Cooking with fresh herbs is only one of the ways you can use your herbs, but if you don't know other ways to prepare and use your herbs, you will waste a lot of herbs. There are so many ways to use your herbs, and in this chapter, I will break down how to dry herbs to use them later, store and infuse fresh herbs, make herbal tea, tinctures, oil extracts, and infuse herbs in honey and vinegar. Using any of these preparations will allow you to get the most out of your herbs and reduce how many you will need to throw onto the compost pile.

Drying Herbs

Drying herbs is one of the best options for reducing herb waste and allowing you to cook with your herbs for longer. The act of drying herbs has been around since ancient times. Through winter months or bad harvesting years, dried herbs still allowed families and cities access to herbs. Nowadays, we can go to the store and buy herbs, but you might have too much when growing your own at home. Drying allows you to preserve herbs and use them later.

As with harvesting, you need to know when to pick your herbs, even drying them. Harvest herbs to dry before the plant's flowers bloom. Pick your herbs on warm mornings after the dew has evaporated.

There are four methods of drying you can choose from, and they are rack, hanging, oven, and microwave drying.

Rack Drying

This method will require a little bit of construction before starting to dry. You will need to construct a wooden frame. You will then want to cover the structure with a muslin cloth, cheesecloth, or netting. Lay the plants on this rack and ensure it is in a warm, dry spot away from direct sunlight. This drying method will take about two to three days, and you should turn the leaves to make sure they are drying evenly.

Hanging Drying

The hanging drying method is commonly used for drying flowers and other plants. You are going to tie together the branches or sprigs of your herbs. Make sure you tie them into small bundles, only a few sprigs or branches. If you tie too many together, mold and discoloration can develop as they will not dry quickly. Hang each bundle with the leaves facing downwards and cover with a thin paper bag or a muslin cloth. Covering them in a muslin cloth or paper bag blocks any dust from collecting but will also catch any seeds or leaves that will fall off. Never wrap your plants in plastic while drying, as it will cause molding. Test the dryness by crushing a leaf. If it sounds crispy when crushed, your herbs are dried. This drying method will take about seven to ten days to complete.

Oven Drying

Set your oven to the lowest temperature possible. Strip the leaves of mint, sage, rosemary, parsley, and thyme when oven drying. The higher the temperature, the more essential oil you will lose from the leaves. If safe to do so, line a baking sheet with muslin. You can also use parchment paper. Space out your leaves evenly and place them in the oven. Keep the oven door open so moisture does not build up, and turn leaves over every 30 minutes. After an hour, the leaves should be dry, but if not, continue to dry. Once dry, turn the oven off but leave them in the oven until cool.

Microwave Drying

This drying method is the quickest and is best for drying small quantities of herbs. You do not want to dry a large batch of herbs at once because they will not dry evenly if you harvest many herbs; either dry small batches at a time or choose to go for oven drying.

Remove the leaves from the stems and rinse them if necessary. You would want to rinse your leaves if you used pesticides in your garden or if the leaves looked dirty. Cover a plate with a paper towel and lay a single layer of herbs on top. Cover with another piece of paper towel and microwave for one minute on high. After a minute, continue to dry at 30-second intervals until the herbs are completely dry. Watch for the smell of burning herbs and stop immediately if you do.

How to Store Dried Herbs

After you have dried your herbs, you need to store them properly, or they will go to waste. After your herbs are dried, you can store them as they are or crumble them, making sure to remove the leafstalks and the midribs of the leaves. Store your dried herbs in an air-tight container. If your containers are clear, make sure they stay out of direct sunlight.

Here are some tips to consider when storing your dried herbs:

- Keeping the herbs whole will give you a stronger flavor when cooking. If you can, store your herbs whole. If not, recognize that the flavor won't be as strong, and you will want to add more.
- Make sure that your herbs are completely dry before storing them. Test by crumbling them in your finger; they are dry enough to crumble easily and are crispy. If not, then continue to dry them.
- Avoid using plastic containers as they can break down and leak chemicals after a specific time.
- Direct sunlight can damage your dried herbs. Keep them out of light or use dark-colored containers.
- Somewhere cool and dry will be the best location to store your herbs.
- Label your herb containers with the type of herb, the date you harvested them, and the date you should discard them. The shelf life could differ from one to three years, depending on the herb. Dried herbs will never go rotten, but eventually, they will lose potency.

How to Store Fresh Herbs

You do not need to dry herbs to store them. You aren't going to be able to store fresh herbs for nearly as long as dried herbs, but adequately storing them can make them last longer and allow you to use fresh herbs in multiple preparations.

To store fresh herbs and get the most extended shelf life out of them, follow these steps:

1. Wash your herbs. The best way to wash your herbs is to put them in a salad spinner with cold water and gently swirl them in the water to loosen any debris that might be stuck on the leaves or stems.
2. Drain the water from the salad spinner and spin until the herbs appear dry. To ensure they are dry, lay on a paper towel and gently pat them to remove any moisture.
3. Hardy herbs such as rosemary, thyme, chives, and sage need to be rolled in a paper towel that has been dampened slightly and stored in plastic wrap or zipper-lock plastic bag and stored in the fridge.
4. Tender herbs such as parsley, dill, cilantro, tarragon, and mint, need to have all discolored leaves removed and the bases of the stems cut. Put an inch of water into a mason jar and place the herbs inside. If the herbs are short enough, close the lid. If not, cover with a plastic bag and seal with an elastic band. Store these herbs in the fridge.
5. Basil is the one herb you won't store in the fridge. Like tender herbs, you will fill a mason jar with about an inch or two of water and snip the base of the stems. Place a bunch of basil in

the jar, but do not cover it. Store at room temperature and in an area with indirect sunlight.

When you store your herbs properly, they will have a longer shelf life than you think. Here is the typical shelf life of some of the herbs you might grow in your garden:

- parsley = three weeks
- tarragon = three weeks
- rosemary = three weeks
- dill = two weeks
- mint = two weeks
- basil = two weeks
- thyme = two weeks
- sage = two weeks
- chives = one week

Infusions with Fresh Herbs

The most popular infusions we see are with water. They can be costly when buying from grocery stores, and instead of wasting your money, you can make infused water at home using the fresh herbs from your garden. The best part of making your infusions at home is saving money, but you can customize them however you like. For many, drinking water can become very difficult because they want something flavored. Learning to infuse your water can boost the flavor you want and ensure you are drinking the water you need to get through the day.

There are numerous ways to infuse your water,

including herbal, floral, spice, and fruit or vegetable. To make your herbal infusions at home, follow these steps:

1. Place two cups of your herbs of choice into a large container and add eight cups of water. If you don't want to make this much infusion, you can divide the recipe.
2. Put a lid on the container and shake. You can split the recipe into smaller containers to make it easier to prepare.
3. Leave the container in the sun for five to eight hours if you want a solid herbal flavor. Store in the fridge and let steep for five to eight hours for a mild herbal taste. Remember, the longer you let the herbs steep, the more flavor infused into the water.
4. Strain water if you desire and throw the waste into your compost.

Another type of infusion you can make that is quick and easy is herbal tea.

Herbal Tea

Herbal teas are some of the best ways to get health benefits from their herbs. In the last chapter, many of the herbs that we discussed had medicinal uses from the tea made from the herbs, such as relieving stress and anxiety or even helping with sleep. Making herbal tea is essentially a sped-up version of infusing water, as you will use dried herbs and hot water to extract the flavor quickly.

Per cup of water, you will use one teaspoon to one tablespoon of herbs. You can pour them directly into the water, use an infuser (best for single cups), a tea ball, or buy empty tea bags and fill them with your dry herbs. After boiling your water, add the herbs and let steep for three to five minutes. The longer they steep, the more intense the flavor. However, make sure you are not over brewing as it can cause the tea to become bitter.

Herbal teas, like infusions can be customized. You don't need just to use one herb. You can use as many as you want and add other ingredients, such as fruit, flowers, or spices, to the mix. If you prefer iced teas over hot, then after brewing, remove the dried herbs, so they do not continue to steep, and place your tea in the fridge to cool.

When making herbal teas, be mindful of the effects the herbs will have and how this can differ depending on how low you steep your tea. Chamomile is a perfect example of the effects of the herbs changing if you steep for an extended period. When steeped for five or fewer minutes,

Chamomile will have a relaxing effect and, help relieve stress anxiety, and even encourage sleep. But if you steep for longer than five minutes, it will become a tonic and have an energizing effect.

Herb Powder

This is a step above drying herbs as it transforms them into powder rather than just pieces of dried herbs. This method is perfect for anyone that doesn't want to have bits of herbs in their meal or would like to add herbs into meals or recipes where they usually would not be. Making herb powder is best for tender herbs such as dill, cilantro, basil, and tarragon.

To make herb powder, set your oven to how low it can go, place herbs on a wire rack, and bake for an hour to an hour and a half. The herbs should be dry and brittle to the touch. Grind the herbs until they are a fine powder and store them in an air-tight container. Herb powder can be kept for a month or so.

There are numerous uses for herb powder, including:

- Herbal shots: mix 20 grams of powder with 50 grams of liquid of choice and take in the morning for a boost of nutrients.
- Add to smoothies for added nutrients. It can be sweetened using honey, agave, and bananas, amongst other things.
- Herbal butter: you can add to nut butter or honey butter and put on toast.

- Add herbal powder to oils and make it into salad dressing or even oil for skin and hair.
- You can use powder as a seasoning in dishes.

Tinctures

Tinctures were briefly brought up in the last chapter, but what exactly are they? Tinctures are used for medicinal purposes and are a mixture of alcohol or water and alcohol with your herb of choice. These will take longer to make, about a couple of weeks or months.

Before making a tincture, perform the body scan exercise.

Body scanning is a meditational practice where you scan your body to see what feels off. This exercise can help you pinpoint specific areas of your body that feel off. If you already have an idea or have been diagnosed with an illness or condition, then this exercise might seem pointless, but it can bring attention to any new issues that might have been hidden behind other pain.

To practice body scanning, sit down in a comfortable position and close your eyes. First, focus on your breathing, feeling how the air leaves and enters your lung. After focusing on the lungs, move to focus on the other parts of the body, taking time to feel the sensation of every limb and any area that might be giving you any discomfort. You can take a little or as long as you need to do this exercise.

After doing this body scan activity, reflect on the herbs you have grown and their medicinal uses. Choose the herbs that best suit your needs.

To make a tincture, you will need:

- your herbs of choice
- a glass jar
- 40% vodka
- cheesecloth
- masking tape
- parchment paper

Follow these steps to make your tincture:

1. Fill your glass jar about halfway with herbs (dry or fresh).
2. Fill with vodka and go about 2 inches above the herbs. Dried herbs will require more vodka down the road.
3. Cover the top of the jar with parchment paper before closing the lid. The parchment paper blocks the alcohol from dissolving the rubber seal.
4. Label the jar using masking tape. Write the date you made the herbs, and the percentage of alcohol.
5. Shake the mixture twice a day for one month.
6. After a month, use the cheesecloth to squeeze out the liquid.

Oil Extract

Oil extract, or infused oil, is a great way to infuse oil you would use for cooking with the properties of your herbs. When making oil extract or infused oil, use plant-based oils such as olive oil, coconut oil, sunflower oil, or almond oil. There are two ways to make oil infusions: solar herbal oil infusion and direct heat herbal oil infusion. There is no set ratio between how much oil and herbs to use for both of these methods. If this is your first time trying oil infusions, try one ounce of dried herbs for every ten ounces of oil.

Use the following steps to make a solar herbal oil infusion:

1. If using fresh herbs, clean if extremely grimy and dry. Excess moisture will ruin the infusion, so be sure your herbs are dry. Skip this step if you are using dried herbs.
2. Add herbs and oil into a jar and seal. Label the jar with the date, the herb, and the type of oil.
3. Place the jar in direct light for 2-3 weeks, stirring daily.
4. After the two to three weeks have passed, strain the herbs and place oil into a dark container and away from any light—the cooler the area, the better the oil's shelf-life. Label the new jar with the date and the infusion.

Use the following steps to make a direct heal oil infusion:

1. In a double boiler, add oil and herbs of your choice.
2. Simmer on low for four to six hours if used for medicinal uses and 30 minutes minimum if only for flavor.
3. Strain the mixture, and put it into a container—label with the date and the type of infusion.

4. Store this mixture in the fridge.

Infusing Herbs in Honey

Infusing herbs in honey is a great practice, especially if you like to use honey to sweeten recipes or teas. It takes longer for honey to adopt some of the flavors of herbs, so give weaker flavored herbs a month to infuse and stronger herbs a minimum of two weeks.

Per cup of honey, add one to two tablespoons of herbs. Stir the honey if need be. When using the honey, remove the herbs. Date the jar and store it with regular honey.

Infusing Herbs in Vinegar

Infusing herbs in vinegar is very similar to water and honey. The type of vinegar is up to you, but some types will react with herbs differently, and it might affect the color. An example of this will be white wine vinegar turning pink if you decide to infuse chive blossoms with it.

To infuse herbs in vinegar, follow these steps:

1. Combine four ounces of dried herbs (double if using fresh) and one pint of vinegar in a jar and label with the date, herb, and type of vinegar.
2. Store in a warm place away from direct sun for two to six weeks.
3. Shake twice a day until the mixture is fine.
4. Strain and throw the herbs into the compost.
5. Pour infused vinegar into a dark container or bottle and store away from direct light. Label

the container with the date and infusion.

There are so many uses for herbs that you might not have initially thought of when starting a garden. When you first started this book, you were likely looking at how to begin gardening, but you have learned so much more than that. You have learned how to grow herbs, maintain them, harvest them, and how you can use them to treat illnesses, diseases, and everyday aches and pains. You have become your gardener, herbalist, physician, and chemist through reading this book. Now it's time to learn how to become your health-conscious chef. In the next chapter, we will discuss cooking with your herbs, and I will give you 22 recipes to try out.

.

Chapter 8: Cooking

Introducing more herbs into your life can happen in many ways, but one of the most popular and easiest ways to do so is to incorporate them into your cooking. To get all the benefits from herbs, such as boosting your health, improving your immune system, and increasing your energy levels, you need to be eating herbs every day. When you are consuming herbs daily and are getting these health benefits, it can prevent you from falling victim to annual sicknesses such as the flu and will overall improve your well-being. This chapter will explore the benefits of using herbs daily, how to use them in your kitchen, and the most common herbs to cook with.

Benefits of Using Herbs Every Day

The biggest reason you should grow herbs is to eat them and get all the health benefits you can from them. We talked about an earlier chapter about the health benefits and the medical uses of herbs. The best way to get these benefits is to eat herbs every day. The benefits of eating an arrangement of herbs every day include:

- maintaining and improving heart health
- increase in antioxidants
- fight and reduce inflammation
- can help to prevent and manage cancer
- can help with weight management

When cooking with herbs, you are likely to use less salt, which helps to improve heart health. Certain herbs also decrease bad cholesterol and blood pressure, which helps to reduce the risk of heart attack and stroke. Herbs that are rich in antioxidants also help to lower cholesterol.

Weight management and eating healthier are great goals that can be helped by eating more herbs. Herbs such as flaxseed, fenugreek, and cinnamon can help control blood sugar and regulate insulin activity, which can aid in managing diabetes and make it easier to lose and maintain weight.

Inflammation occurs when the body is triggered to fight infections and start healing. Usually, the body will return to normal once it is healed. But sometimes, someone can develop chronic inflammation, where the body remains in a state of inflammation long after it has healed. Inflammation is only good for a short period as it triggers the immune system to defend and heal the body. When we are in that state for too long, it can be detrimental to our health, including weakening our immune systems, increasing blood pressure, and increasing the risk for heart disease. Eating more herbs can help to decrease inflammation. To reduce inflammation, eat more ginger, garlic, cardamom, turmeric, ginseng, black pepper, rosemary, green tea, and cinnamon.

Ways to Use Herbs in Your Kitchen Daily

If you are new to herbs, you might not know precisely how to introduce them into your diet. In the last chapter, I talked about numerous ways to infuse different ingredients with herbs. These infusions can be used in cooking, but these aren't the only ways to introduce herbs. Try some of these methods to use herbs in your kitchen daily:

- Add herbs to homemade dressings, vinegarettes, dips, and salads.
- Use dried herbs to season chicken or other meat before roasting.
- Make a marinade with olive oil, fresh or dried herbs, and lemon juice
- Add oregano and basil to spaghetti sauce to give it a flavor boost. This is great for store-bought spaghetti sauce.

- Season your curry with coriander or lemongrass.
- Add mint to fruit salads.
- Use herb sprigs to stuff fish, chicken, or turkey before cooking.
- Top pizzas with parsley or basil.
- Create a mint sauce and roast lamb with rosemary.

Common herbs to use in your cooking include basil, chives, cilantro, dill, mint, oregano, parsley, rosemary, sage, tarragon, and thyme.

Recipes with Herbs

You can add herbs to any of the dishes you make regularly using the methods that I talked about earlier. But if you want to try some new recipes centered around herbs, keep reading to find eight savory recipes and three dessert recipes that will help you eat more herbs.

Spiced Chicken and Cilantro Lime Butter

Ingredients:

Spiced Chicken:

- 6 bone-in chicken breasts, halved
- 3 tablespoons of olive oil
- 1 tablespoon of chili powder
- 1 tablespoon of balsamic vinegar
- 2 teaspoons of brown sugar
- 1/2 teaspoon of salt
- 1/8 teaspoon of pepper

Cilantro-Lime Butter:

- 1 finely chopped serrano pepper
- 1/3 cup of melted butter
- 1/4 cup of cilantro, fresh
- 2 tablespoons of red onion, finely chopped
- 1 tablespoon of lemon juice
- 1/8 teaspoon of pepper

Instructions:

1. Combine seasonings, oil, and vinegar, and brush over chicken breasts.
2. Cook chicken in any manner you like until done.
3. As the chicken is cooking, combine the ingredients for the cilantro-lime butter.

4. Drizzle butter over the chicken before serving.

Herbed Feta Dip

Ingredients:

- 4 cups of feta cheese, crumbled
- 1/2 cup of mint leaves, fresh
- 1/2 cup of parsley sprigs, fresh and packed
- 1/2 cup of olive oil
- 2 garlic cloves
- 3 tablespoons of lemon juice
- 1/2 teaspoon of pepper
- your choice of assorted vegetables

Instructions:

1. Combine parsley, mint, olive oil, garlic cloves, and pepper in a food processor until everything is finely chopped.
2. Add lemon juice and cheese and pulse until the mixture is creamy.
3. Serve with your assortment of vegetables.

Rosemary Focaccia

Ingredients:

- 3-4 cups of all-purpose flour
- 1 1/2 cup of warm water (temperature around 110-115 degrees)
- 1/4 cup and 3 tablespoons of olive oil
- 2 onions, chopped

- 2 tablespoons of fresh rosemary or 2 teaspoons of dried rosemary
- 1 1/2 teaspoons of active dry yeast
- 1/2 teaspoon of salt
- 1/2 teaspoon of sugar
- coarse salt
- cornmeal

Instructions:

1. Heat 1/4 cup of oil and add onions. Cook for six to eight minutes or until tender.
2. Add yeast and 1/4 cup of water to a large bowl and dissolve. Add sugar and let sit for five minutes. Add remaining water, two tablespoons of oil, and salt and stir. Add two cups of flour and stir until a dough forms.
3. Sprinkle a layer of flour on the counter and knead the dough for about six to eight minutes or until elastic and smooth. Add the cooked onions and half of the rosemary and knead for another minute.
4. Grease a bowl and place dough inside, flipping it once to allow all the dough to be greased. Cover and let rest for 40 minutes.
5. Punch dough down and divide it in half on a floured surface. Gently flatten and let sit for another five minutes. Sprinkle greased baking sheets with cornmeal. Stretch dough into 10-inch circles and place onto pans. Cover again and let rise for 40 minutes.

6. Preheat the oven to 375 degrees Fahrenheit.
7. Use the remaining oil to brush onto the dough. Sprinkle remaining rosemary and coarse salt on top and bake for 25-30 minutes.

Herb Butter

Ingredients:

- 1/2 cup of softened butter
- 1 1/2 teaspoon of fresh tarragon, minced
- 1 1/2 teaspoon of fresh chives, minced
- 1/2 teaspoon of garlic powder

Instructions:

1. Beat butter, herbs, and garlic powder together until it is all blended.

This butter can be served with biscuits, and crackers, or used as a marinade for meat.

Cheddar and Chive Mashed Potatoes

Ingredients:

- 5 pounds of potatoes (Yukon Gold recommended), peeled and cut
- 1 1/2 cup of Monterey Jack cheese, shredded
- 1 1/2 cup of cheddar cheese, shredded
- 1 cup of sour cream
- 1 cup of cubed butter
- 1/2 cup of heavy whipping cream

- 1/4 cup of Parmesan cheese
- 2 tablespoons of fresh chives, minced
- 2 teaspoons of salt
- 3/4 teaspoons of pepper

Toppings:

- 6 ounces or one can of french-fried onions
- 1 cup of cheddar cheese, shredded

Instructions:

1. Cook potatoes until tender. Drain and transfer into a large bowl.
2. Add pepper, salt, butter, and sour cream into the bowl with potatoes. Beat the mixture until everything is blended.
3. Add whipping cream and beat until incorporated.
4. Stir in chives and cheese.
5. Place in a baking dish and refrigerate overnight.
6. Preheat oven to 350 degrees and back for 45 minutes, covered.
7. Stir after 30 minutes and add toppings. Bake for another 15 minutes.

Green Beans with Fresh Herbs

Ingredients:

- 1 pound of green beans, fresh
- 2 tablespoons each of fresh parsley, cilantro, and mint, minced

- 2 tablespoons of olive oil
- 2 minced garlic cloves
- 1/2 teaspoon of salt
- 1/4 teaspoon of pepper

Instructions:

1. Heat oil over medium heat, and then add garlic—Cook for one minute.
2. Add salt, pepper, and green beans. Stir to coat and then cook covered for 8-10 minutes, stirring occasionally.
3. Add herbs and cook for another 1-2 minutes.

Cilantro Lime Shrimp

Ingredients:

- 1 pound of peeled, deveined, and uncooked shrimp
- 1/3 cup of lime juice
- 1/3 cup of fresh cilantro, chopped
- 3 minced garlic cloves
- 1 jalapeno, minced and seeded
- 1 1/2 teaspoons of lime zest, grated
- 1/4 teaspoon of ground cumin
- 1/4 teaspoon of salt
- 1/4 teaspoon of pepper
- lime slices

Instructions:

1. Toss shrimp in cilantro, lime zest, lime juice, jalapeno, olive oil, garlic cloves, salt, ground

cumin, and pepper.
2. Let the shrimp stand for 15 minutes.
3. On oven-safe skewers, thread lime slices and shrimp. Grill over medium heat for about 2-4 minutes per side or until shrimp becomes pink.

Dill Cheesy Ball

Ingredients:

- 8 ounces or one package of cream cheese
- 1 1/2 cup of cheddar cheese, shredded
- 1 cup of drained dill pickle relish
- 1/4 cup of onion, finely chopped
- 2 tablespoons of fresh parsley, minced
- 2 tablespoons of mayonnaise
- 1 tablespoon of Worcestershire sauce

Instructions:

1. Combine cream cheese, dill pickle relish, onion, cheddar cheese, Worcestershire sauce, and mayonnaise.
2. Shape mixture into a ball, cover in plastic wrap, and refrigerate for several hours.
3. Sprinkle with parsley and serve with crackers and vegetables.

Cinnamon Basil Ice Cream

You will need an ice cream maker for this recipe.

Ingredients:

- 12 basil leaves
- 4 large eggs
- 1 1/4 cups of whole milk
- 3/4 cup of heavy whipping cream
- 1/2 cup of sugar
- 1/4 teaspoon of vanilla extract
- 1 cinnamon stick
- optional: ground cinnamon

Instructions:

1. Warm milk to 175 degrees. Remove milk from heat and add the cinnamon stick and basil.
2. Cover pan and steep for 30 minutes.
3. Strain and throw out basil and cinnamon.
4. Return steeped milk back onto the heat and add sugar, stirring until dissolved. Lightly beat eggs and add small amounts to milk and egg mixture at a time.
5. Continue to cook over light heat. Stir constantly until the mixture is thick and coats a spoon.
6. Remove from heat when the mixture reaches 160 degrees.
7. Transfer mix into a bowl and place bowl into ice water. Stir gently for five minutes or until the mixture is cooled. Stir in vanilla extract and cream.
8. Cover with plastic wrap and refrigerate overnight or a minimum of several hours.
9. Use the ice cream maker as per instructions and refrigerate any mix that doesn't fit. You should only fill your ice cream maker about two-thirds

full.
10. Put ice cream in the freezer and freeze for about 2-4 hours before eating. If you wish, you can sprinkle the ice cream with cinnamon before eating.

Peach Basil Lemonade Slush

Ingredients:

- 5-8 cups of ice cubes
- 4 cups of water
- 3 cups of fresh peaches, peeled and chopped
- 2 cups of sugar
- 1 1/2 cups of fresh lemon juice
- 20 large basil leaves or one package of fresh basil leaves

Instructions:

1. Bring sugar, water, peaches, and basil to a boil—lower heat and simmer for five minutes.
2. Remove from heat and let sit for 30 minutes. Remove basil and add lemon juice.
3. Refrigerate until the mixture is completely cooled.
4. In a blender, add half of the peach mixture with 2 1/2 cups of ice. Blend until smooth, and add more ice if you desire. Repeat the process with the remaining peach mixture.
5. Serve in cooled glasses and garnish with basil and peaches if you desire.

Frozen Strawberry-Basil Margarita

Ingredients:

- 1 cup of frozen strawberries, sliced
- 4 basil leaves
- 1 1/2 ounces of Blanco tequila
- 1 ounce of triple sec
- 1/2 ounce of lime juice, freshly squeezed
- 1 lime wedge
- optional: coarse sugar and fresh strawberries

Instructions:

1. Run lime wedge over the rim of a glass and dip into sugar, if desired.
2. Blend tequila, lime juice, strawberries, and basil until smooth.
3. Pour into a glass and garnish with a lime wedge and fresh strawberries if you want.

Vegan Recipes with Herbs

There is often the stigma that vegan food is bland and not flavorful. But this is false. Here are eight savory and three vegan dessert recipes that are anything but boring and chock-full of herbs.

Vegan Almond Cheese and Garlic Herb Spread

Ingredients:

- 1 cup of almonds, raw and whole

- 1/2 cup of water
- 1/4 cup of your choice of fresh herbs, finely chopped
- 2 tablespoons of nutritional yeast
- 2 tablespoons of lemon juice
- 1 tablespoon of olive oil
- 1/2 teaspoon of salt
- 1/2 teaspoon of garlic powder

Instructions:

1. Soak almonds for 24 hours and refrigerate.
2. Drain and rinse almonds.
3. Blend almonds, lemon juice, water, nutritional yeast, olive oil, salt, and garlic powder until smooth.
4. Add herbs and mix evenly.
5. Store in an airtight container and refrigerate for at least a few hours. You can keep this dip stored unused for up to four or five days.

Zhoug Sauce

Ingredients:

- 2 cups of cilantro
- 1 1/4 cups of walnut halves, raw
- 3 garlic cloves
- 2-3 jalapenos
- 3-5 tablespoons of water
- 2 tablespoons of fresh lemon or lime juice
- 3/4-1 teaspoon of sea salt

- 1/2-1 teaspoon of red pepper flakes
- 1/2-3/4 teaspoon of ground cardamom
- 1/2 teaspoon of ground cumin

Instructions:

1. Remove jalapeno seeds for a lower heat level, keep some for a high spice level, and slice jalapenos.
2. In a food processor, blend garlic, jalapenos, and walnuts until the texture is crumbly and sticky. Add red pepper flakes, cilantro, cumin, lemon/lime juice, salt, and cardamom. Blend until everything is finely chopped.
3. Add water, one tablespoon at a time, and continue to blend until you reach your desired consistency.

Parsley Dill Pesto

Ingredients:

- 1 cup of fresh parsley, chopped
- 1/2 cup of pumpkin seeds, raw
- 1/2 cup of walnuts, raw
- 1/2 cup of fresh dill, chopped
- 2 garlic cloves
- 2 tablespoons of lemon juice
- 2 tablespoons of nutritional yeast
- 1/2 teaspoon of salt
- 1-3 tablespoons of oil or water (optional)

Instructions:

1. Combine all ingredients into a food processor and blend until everything is smooth.
2. If you choose to add some oil and water, slowly drizzle it in and mix until incorporated.

Quinoa Salad with Herbs

Ingredients:

- 1 cup of quinoa, uncooked
- 7.5 ounces of tofu of choice
- 1 cucumber
- 1/2 of an onion
- 1/2 cup of kalamata olives, chopped

Dressing:

- 2 cups of spinach, fresh
- 1 cup of parsley, fresh
- 1 cup of cilantro, fresh
- 1/4 cup of tahini
- 1 garlic cloves
- one piece of fresh ginger
- juice of one lemon
- salt and pepper

Instructions:

1. Cube tofu, peel and cube cucumber, dice onions, and chop olive. Place prepared foods in a bowl.
2. Blend all dressing ingredients until smooth. To

thin out the mixture, add water.
3. Toss salad in dressing and serve.

Rosemary Cauliflower Mash

Ingredients:

- 1 head of cauliflower
- 3 tablespoons of vegan butter
- 1-2 tablespoons of non-dairy milk, unsweetened
- 1 teaspoon of fresh rosemary, chopped
- salt and pepper
- 1 teaspoon of champagne vinegar (optional)

Instructions:

1. Cut cauliflower into small-sized florets and steam cauliflower with a sprinkle of salt and rosemary.
2. Drain any water from the cauliflower and place it in a food processor. Add salt, pepper, butter, milk, and vinegar to the cauliflower and blend until smooth.

Veggie and Herbs Burritos

Ingredients:

- 4 cups of quinoa or salad, cooked
- 14 ounces of drained and rinsed pinto beans
- 2 cups of cabbage, shredded
- 1 1/2 cup of salsa or pico degallo
- 1 bunch of cilantro, chopped

- 4 flour tortillas
- 1 avocado
- salt and pepper
- lime juice, to taste

Instructions:

1. Cook rice or quinoa.
2. Peel, pit, and mash avocado. Mix with lime juice, salt, and pepper.
3. Drain and rinse beans and then warm over medium heat in a skillet.
4. Rinse cilantro and dry well. Remove 1 inch of the stems and finely chop.
5. Warm tortillas and fill with rice, avocado, cilantro, and cabbage. Wrap and enjoy.

Jackfruit, Mango, and Dill Salad

Ingredients:

- 20 ounces or one can of green jackfruit in brine
- 1 poblano pepper
- 1 mango
- 1/4 to 1/3 cup of vegan Mayonnaise
- 1/4 cup of minced shallots
- 1 1/2 tablespoon of grapeseed oil
- 1 tablespoon of dill, chopped
- 1/2 lemon zest and juice
- salt and pepper to taste

Instructions:

1. Drain and rinse jackfruit well. Let jackfruit sit in water for a few minutes and drain to reduce the brine flavor. Gather jackfruit into a towel and squeeze out any liquid. Tear the jackfruit into bite-size pieces. If there are any tough pieces, especially near the core, discard these.
2. Preheat the oven to 425 degrees. Grease the baking sheet with one tablespoon of oil and roast pepper for six to eight minutes, flip and roast for another six to eight minutes. Place roasted pepper in a bowl and cover. Let steam in the bowl for five to ten minutes. Peel, remove seeds and cut the stem off. Set pepper to the side.
3. Add a tablespoon of oil and jackfruit into a pan and warm over medium heat. Cook for three to five minutes, stirring, so the jackfruit is covered in oil. Add a couple of tablespoons of water and cover to steam for 2-3 minutes. Add salt and lemon juice, stirring to coat the jackfruit. Remove mixture from heat and let cool.
4. Toss jackfruit, mayo, lemon zest, pepper, shallots, and dill in a bowl. Season with salt, pepper, and mayo if you desire.
5. Peel and slice mango and top salad.

Baked Farro with Herbs and Tomatoes

Ingredients:

- 2 cups of farro, uncooked

- 28 ounces of canned diced tomatoes
- 2 cups of vegetable broth, low-sodium
- 1/2 cup of fresh parsley or basil, chopped
- 1/2 cup of shallots, chopped
- 2 garlic cloves
- 2 tablespoons of olive oil
- 2 tablespoons of nutritional yeast
- 1 teaspoon of dried basil or thyme
- 1/2 teaspoon of salt
- 1 bay leaf

Walnut Topping:

- 1/4 cup of nutritional yeast
- 1/4 cup of walnuts, chopped
- 2 tablespoons of olive oil
- 1/2 teaspoon of lemon zest, grated
- 1/2 teaspoon of salt

Instructions:

1. Preheat the oven to 350 degrees Fahrenheit and grease a baking dish with one tablespoon of oil.
2. Rinse farro.
3. Saute shallot and garlic with one tablespoon of olive oil for about two minutes or until the shallot is soft. Add bay leaf and farro and saute for one minute. Add tomatoes and vegetable broth.
4. Bring to a rapid simmer and cook for two minutes. Remove from heat and add thyme, oregano, and salt. Remove bay leaf, and season more if desired.

Stir in nutritional yeast and parsley.
5. Transfer farro into baking dish and cover with tin foil. Bake for 40 minutes or until most of the liquid has been absorbed.
6. Prepare walnut topping by adding all ingredients except olive oil to a food processor and blending until it forms a crumble.
7. Remove dish from oven and top with walnut topping and drizzle two tablespoons on top. Bake for another ten minutes.
8. Sit to allow the mixture to firm before serving.

Mango and Mint Smoothie

Ingredients:

- 2 cups of mango chunks, frozen
- 1 small banana, (you can use another fruit or sweetener as well)
- 6-7 mint leaves, the larger, the better
- 1 cup of vegan yogurt, unsweetened
- 1/2 cup of non-dairy milk, unsweetened
- 1 tablespoon of lime juice, fresh

Instructions:

1. Combine milk, lime juice, mango, and yogurt in a blender.
2. Add a banana or other sweetener if desired and mint leaves. Blend until smooth.

Rosemary and Tahini Cookies

Ingredients:

- 3/4 cup of oat flour
- 1/2 cup of tahini
- 1/2 cup of coconut sugar
- 1/4 cup of rolled oats
- 2 tablespoons of non-dairy milk
- 1 tablespoon of maple syrup
- 1 tablespoon of fresh rosemary, chopped
- 1 teaspoon of vanilla extract
- 1/2 teaspoon of baking soda
- 1/4 teaspoon of sea salt
- 3-4 tablespoons of chocolate chips (optional)

Instructions:

1. Use parchment paper to line a baking sheet and preheat your oven to 370 degrees Fahrenheit.
2. Whisk together oats, oat flour, sea salt, and baking soda.
3. In a separate bowl, combine coconut sugar, maple syrup, tahini, and the majority of the rosemary. Add this mixture with the dry ingredients and mix.
4. Add chocolate chips if you want.
5. Scoop about 1 1/2 tablespoons of the cookie dough and place it on a baking sheet. Slightly flatten the cookies with the palm of your hand and press a few pieces of rosemary on top of each cookie.
6. Bake for 10-12 minutes or until the cookies are

golden brown.
7. Let cool for five minutes before moving them onto a cooling rack.

Thyme and Raspberry Gin Cocktail

Ingredients:

- 8 raspberries, fresh
- juice from half a lemon
- 1-2 teaspoons of agave
- 1 teaspoon of thyme leaves, fresh
- 2 shots of water
- 1 shot of gin

Instructions:

1. Muddle raspberries and thyme before adding the other ingredients.
2. Shake or stir to incorporate ingredients.
3. Serve with lots of ice.

When cooking with herbs, have fun and experiment. Throughout your entire herb gardening journey, remember always to have fun. When you are too hard on yourself, you will start to stress. Gardening and cooking are supposed to be activities where you have fun and explore. Remember that herbs, in part, will be filled with the love and energy that you put into them. Enjoy the process of growing your herbs, harvesting them, and finally being able to eat them and get all the health benefits you can. We are reaching the end of this journey, but before it ends, let's recap what we have learned before you start enjoying herbs to the fullest and becoming healthier and happier as you do.

Conclusion

We are reaching the end of our journey together, but there is no need to fret. You have learned so much up to this point, and now you can start growing your medicinal herbs and reaping all the benefits from them. Throughout this book, you've learned what it takes to begin gardening, how to grow herbs, maintain them, use them in your kitchen and medicinally, and how to make food and medicinal products from your herbs.

Gardening and consuming herbs have unprecedented benefits for your mental and physical health. The act of spending time caring for your plants and gardening is great for improving mood, relieving stress and anxiety, and decreasing depression. Eating herbs regularly helps to improve physical health by increasing antioxidants, improving heart health, maintaining weight, reducing inflammation, helping to prevent and manage cancer, and so much more.

Growing your medicinal herbs means you do not need to rely on anyone to become the healthiest version of yourself. Depending on the medicinal herbs you grow, you can treat any underlying health conditions or illnesses and boost your immune system so that you never have to fight with any such as the flu.

The most significant benefit of growing your medicinal herbs is the thousands of dollars you can save annually. The massive health benefits you get from growing and consuming herbs means you won't need to spend money on practitioners, doctors, and medications. Eating more herbs allows you to fix the root problem and boost your overall health.

It's now in your hands to take the first steps and start your garden. It is time for you to take the steps necessary to improve yourself. You cannot begin to reducing inflammation and improving your health unless you take steps to create a plan for yourself and actively decide to change your life for the better. Changing your life and starting your herbal garden does not only mean that you can improve your health, but you can also help your loved ones to become healthier versions of themselves.

It's time for you to start your journey, and let's spread this knowledge together. Leaving a review can help others get insights into how much this book can change their lives. Assisting others to feel amazing, and if this book helped you, please take a minute to leave a review to know the success and happiness you have found. Let's help humanity to grow together!

References

24 Mantra. (2020). *Coriander and its medicinal uses.* 24 Mantra. https://www.24mantra.com/blogs/health-and-nutrition/medicinal-uses-of-coriander-leaves-seeds-and-extracts/

Academy of Culinary Nutrition. (2017, November 30). *Guide to homemade medicine: healing tinctures and tonics.* Academy of Culinary Nutrition. https://www.culinarynutrition.com/how-to-make-tinctures-and-tonics/

AEssenseGrows. (n.d.). *Garlic chives.* AEssenseGrows. Retrieved January 20, 2022, from https://www.aessensegrows.com/en/fresh-produce-catalog/garlic_chives#:~:text=Garlic%20chives%20are%20rich%20in

Alex. (2021, May 29). Low-maintenance *herbs that will survive anything.* Homegrown Herb Garden. https://homegrownherbgarden.com/2021/05/29/low-maintenance-herbs-that-will-survive-anything/

Almanac Editors. (n.d.). *Lavender.* Almanac. Retrieved

January 21, 2022, from https://www.almanac.com/plant/lavender#:~:text=How%20to%20Care%20for%20Lavender

Anderson, M. K. (2017, March 23). *The original medicinal plant gatherers & conservationists.* United Plant Savers. https://unitedplantsavers.org/the-original-medicinal-plant-gatherers-conservationists/

Anderson, Samee (2020). *Food photography of herbs and seasonings* [Online Photo]. Unsplash. https://unsplash.com/photos/3tBdYnx_sWA

Andreas. (2020, May 21). *23 main pros & cons of greenhouse farming.* E&C. https://environmental-conscience.com/greenhouses-pros-cons/

Andrychowicz, A. (2019, July 26). *How to fertilize herbs in the organic garden.* Get Busy Gardening. https://getbusygardening.com/fertilizing-herbs/

Barclay Friends. (2020, June 22). *The many benefits of gardening.* Barclay Friends. https://bf.kendal.org/2020/06/22/the-many-benefits-of-gardening/#:~:text=Physical%20Benefits&text=The%20pulling%2C%20digging%2C%20reaching%2C

Better Homes & Gardens. (2016). *Planting potted herbs.* Better Homes & Gardens. https://www.bhg.com/gardening/vegetable/herbs/planting-potted-herbs/

Binley Florist and Garden Center. (n.d.). *Types of herb*

gardens. Binley Florist and Garden Center. Retrieved January 9, 2022, from https://www.binleyflorist.com/herbs-information/78-types-of-herb-gardens

Biodynamic Association. (2019). *Who was Rudolf Steiner?* Biodynamic Association. https://www.biodynamics.com/steiner.html

Blankespoor, J. (2012, December 13). *Lavender's medicinal and aromatherapy uses*. Chestnut School of Herbal Medicine. https://chestnutherbs.com/lavenders-medicinal-and-aromatherapy-uses-and-lavender-truffles/#:~:text=Lavender%20is%20applied%20topically%20on

Bonnie Plants. (2020, January 22). *How to harvest herbs*. YouTube. https://www.youtube.com/watch?v=_EL3pnnLs6c

Buckner, H. (2020, March 25). *The uses and benefits of yarrow*. Gardener's Path. https://gardenerspath.com/plants/herbs/yarrow-benefits-uses/#Medicinal-Use-and-Potential-Health-Benefits

Butler, N. (2018). *Stevia: Health benefits, facts, and safety*. Medical News Today. https://www.medicalnewstoday.com/articles/287251#Possible-health-benefits

Caldwell, M. (2020). How and when to cover plants during cold weather. *The Atlanta Journal-Constitution*.

https://www.ajc.com/things-to-do/atlanta-winter-guide/how-and-when-to-cover-plants-during-cold-weather/GMGIMANNWYMLLVJ3GS7YMWNZVY/

Carmen. (2011, May 16). *Using oregano medicinally*. Off the Grid News. https://www.offthegridnews.com/alternative-health/using-oregano-medicinally/

Carruthers, D. (2020, April 29). *Top 10 greenhouse tools & equipment*. Cultivar Greenhouse. https://www.cultivargreenhouses.co.uk/inspiration/greenhouse-tools-equipment

CeAnne. (2021). *How to harvest herbs efficiently - top 5 harvest tools*. Grow Create Sip. https://www.growcreatesip.com/blog/herb-harvest-tools

Chase, A. R. (n.d.). *Herbs: Your worst enemies*. Greenhouse Product News. Retrieved January 14, 2022, from https://gpnmag.com/article/herbs-your-worst-enemies/

Chen, Eleanor (2020). *Mint* [Online Photo]. Unsplash. https://unsplash.com/photos/IytUViSv3GQ

Codekas, C. (2016, August 5). *6 tips for storing dried herbs*. Herbal Academy. https://theherbalacademy.com/6-tips-for-storing-dried-herbs/

Col, Marcus Dall (2017). *Planet photo* [Online Photo]. Unsplash. https://unsplash.com/photos/6RMFM8uv3eY

Community Servings Food Heals. (2016). *Nutrition*

spotlight: The health benefits of herbs & spices. Community Servings Food Heals. https://www.servings.org/about-us/news/nutrition-spotlight-the-health-benefits-of-herbs-spices/#:~:text=Herbs%20and%20spices%20are%20a

Cooking Light. (2004). *11 fresh herbs every home cook should use.* Cooking Light. https://www.cookinglight.com/cooking-101/essential-ingredients/all-about-herbs-slideshow

Czapp, Arpad (2021). *Grapevine Pruning at Czapp Winery* [Online Photo]. Unsplash https://unsplash.com/photos/nebwVFFwTgE

D, J. (2019, August 12). *Light requirements for herbs: What should you know?* Herbs Within. https://herbswithin.com/light-requirements-for-herbs/

D, J. (2020, September 7). *Fertilizer for herbs: Your best options!* Herbs Within. https://herbswithin.com/fertilizer-for-herbs/

Deanna. (2020, January 14). *9 common seed starting mistakes to avoid.* Homestead and Chill. https://homesteadandchill.com/seed-starting-mistakes/

Dellwo, A. (2021). *The health benefits of yarrow.* Verywell Health. https://www.verywellhealth.com/yarrow-health-benefits-4586386

Delude, C. (2012, February 12). *Secrets of ancient Chinese remedy revealed.* Harvard Gazette.

https://news.harvard.edu/gazette/story/2012/02/secrets-of-ancient-chinese-remedy-revealed/

Dyer, M. (2021). *Preparing herbs for winter*. Gardening Know How. https://www.gardeningknowhow.com/edible/herbs/hgen/how-to-overwinter-herbs.htm

EarthEasy. (2019). *Composting*. Eartheasy. https://learn.eartheasy.com/guides/composting/

Eartheasy. (2013). *Know your garden soil: How to make the most of your soil type*. Eartheasy. https://learn.eartheasy.com/articles/know-your-garden-soil-how-to-make-the-most-of-your-soil-type/

Ellis, M. E. (2021). *Uses for dandelions: What to do with dandelions*. Gardening Know How. https://www.gardeningknowhow.com/edible/herbs/dandelion/uses-for-dandelions.htm

eMedicine Health. (n.d.). *Fennel: Uses, side effects, dose, health benefits, precautions & warnings*. EMedicine Health. https://www.emedicinehealth.com/fennel/vitamins-supplements.htm

Environmental Pest Control. (2017, November 7). *What is pest control?* Environmental Pest Control. https://www.environmentalpestcontrol.ca/blog/what-is-pest-control#:~:text=Pest%20control%20is%20the%20process

Erin. (2019, March 11). *How to root plant cuttings in*

water for propagation. Clever Bloom. https://cleverbloom.com/root-plant-cuttings-water/

Family Food Garden. (2017, December 22). *Herb gardening design in permaculture zones*. Family Food Garden. https://www.familyfoodgarden.com/herb-gardening-design-permaculture-garden-zones/

Frey, M. (2021). *Why dill should be your new super herb*. Verywell Fit. https://www.verywellfit.com/dill-benefits-side-effects-and-preparations-4243918

Garden & Greenhouse. (2017). *The importance of consistency in greenhouses and indoor gardens*. Garden & Greenhouse. https://www.gardenandgreenhouse.net/articles/greenhouse-articles/importance-consistency-greenhouses-indoor-gardens/

Garden Myths. (2015, December 1). *Organic seeds - why buy them?* Garden Myths. https://www.gardenmyths.com/organic-seeds-why-buy-them/

Gardener Basics. (n.d.). *Herbs: The ultimate annual and perennial list*. Gardener Basics. Retrieved January 22, 2022, from https://www.gardenerbasics.com/blog/herbs-annual-and-perennial-list

Gardening Channel. (2021, May 19). *What herbs should not be planted together?* Gardening Channel. https://www.gardeningchannel.com/herbs-not-planted-together/

Gilmour. (2017, June 29). *Essential guide to growing herbs - indoors and outdoors*. Gilmour. https://gilmour.com/herb-growing-guide

Grant, A. (2021). *Herb growing problems: Common herb garden pests and diseases*. Gardening Know How. https://www.gardeningknowhow.com/edible/herbs/hgen/herb-growing-problems.htm

Greenhouse Emporium. (2017, February 24). *Greenhouse gardening for beginners - where do I start?* Greenhouse Emporium. https://greenhouseemporium.com/blogs/greenhouse-gardening/greenhouse-gardening-for-beginners/

Green, Viridi (2020). *Yellow flower with green leaves* [Online Photo]. Unsplash. https://unsplash.com/photos/i-uBAOo_BBA

Griffin, R. M. (2021). *Chamomile health benefits & uses*. WebMD. https://www.webmd.com/diet/supplement-guide-chamomile

Groves, M. N. (n.d.). *When and how to harvest herbs for medicinal use*. Storey Publishing. https://www.storey.com/article/harvest-herbs-medicinal-use/

Grow a Good Life. (2020, February 20). *7 simple technique to improve garden soil*. Grow a Good Life. https://growagoodlife.com/improve-garden-soil/

Grow Organic. (2018). *How to make your own high-quality compost*. Grow Organic. https://www.groworganic.com/blogs/articles/how-to-make-your-own-high-quality-compost-for-compost-tea

Guha, A. (2016). *Where does ayurveda come from?* Taking Charge of Your Health & Wellbeing. https://www.takingcharge.csh.umn.edu/where-ayurveda-come-from

H., Paulina (2020). *Green plant on white textile* [Online Photo]. Unsplash. https://unsplash.com/photos/4jnzsIB9vbg

Habas, C. (2021). *Herbs that don't like being planted together*. SF Gate. https://homeguides.sfgate.com/herbs-dont-like-being-planted-together-40828.html

Hagen, L. (2019). *12 gardening tools to buy - essentials for beginners*. Garden Design. https://www.gardendesign.com/how-to/tools.html

Hansen, J. (n.d.). *How to grow container herbs both indoors and outside*. Garden Tech. Retrieved January 10, 2022, from https://www.gardentech.com/blog/how-to-guides/easy-herbs-for-indoors-and-out

Healthy Food Guide. (2016, September 27). *How to include herbs in everyday cooking*. Healthy Food Guide. https://www.healthyfood.com/advice/how-to-include-herbs-in-everyday-cooking/

Healthy Slow Cooking. (2021, June 6). *Fresh raspberry gin cocktail with thyme*. Healthy Slow Cooking. https://healthyslowcooking.com/end-of-summer-raspberry-cocktail/

Herbs. (2012). Vic.gov.au. https://www.betterhealth.vic.gov.au/health/healthyliving/herbs

Hicks Nurseries. (2014, July 25). *How to trim your herbs and keep them happy!* Hicks Nurseries. https://hicksnurseries.com/herbs-and-vegetables/how-to-trim-your-herbs-and-keep-them-happy/

Higuera, V. (2019). *What is lavender? Possible health benefits, how to grow it, and best sellers*. Everyday Health. https://www.everydayhealth.com/diet/what-are-possible-benefits-lavender-must-know-facts-about-therapeutic-plant/

Hinck, M. (2018, July 5). *The health benefits of rosemary*. Health Beat. https://www.flushinghospital.org/newsletter/the-health-benefits-of-rosemary/#:~:text=Rosemary%20is%20a%20rich%20source

Hobbs, Lisa (2017). *Tea* [Online Photo]. Unsplash. https://unsplash.com/photos/mRaNok_Ld6s

Home Made Simple. (n.d.). *7 herbs that are surprisingly easy to grow and cook with*. Home Made Simple. Retrieved January 22, 2022, from https://www.homemadesimple.com/kitchen/herbs-that-are-surprisingly-easy-to-grow-and-cook-with/

Homes to Love. (2018). *10 easy to grow herb plants*. Homes to Love. https://www.homestolove.com.au/10-easy-to-grow-herb-plants-3214

Hu, S. (2020, July 20). *Composting* 101. NRDC. https://www.nrdc.org/stories/composting-101

Hutchins, R. (2017, October 31). *8 surprising health benefits of gardening*. UNC Health Talk. https://healthtalk.unchealthcare.org/health-benefits-of-gardening/

Iannotti, M. (2021). *Start seeds indoors for head start on the gardening season*. The Spruce. https://www.thespruce.com/successful-start-seed-indoors-1402478

Indigo Herbs. (n.d.). *How to take a herbal powder*. Indigo Herbs. Retrieved January 23, 2022, from https://www.indigo-herbs.co.uk/natural-health-guide/how-to-take-herbal-powders

Ivanova, Valentine (2019). *Red and yellow tomatoes in brown woven basket* [Online Photo]. Unsplash. https://unsplash.com/photos/mkhohyHMhcc

Jabbour, N. (2021, June 18). *How to harvest herbs: How and when to harvest homegrown herbs*. Savvy Gardening. https://savvygardening.com/how-to-harvest-herbs/

James, Andrew (2018). *Lakota Native American Man at Pow Wow* [Online Photo]. Unsplash.

https://unsplash.com/photos/ehdsg7SHm6A

Jeanroy, A. (2021). *Learn how to prune your herb garden.* The Spruce. https://www.thespruce.com/prune-my-herb-garden-1762505

Jouron, R. (2013). *Problems encountered by home gardeners when growing transplants indoors.* Iowa State University. https://hortnews.extension.iastate.edu/2013/03-08/transplants.html

Joybilee Farm. (2016, August 4). *5 uses for sage and how to make an oxymel.* Joybilee Farm. https://joybileefarm.com/sage-herb/#:~:text=Sage%20can%20be%20enjoyed%20as

Kacerova, Zuzuna (2021). *Brown and black hanging décor* [Online Photo]. Unsplash. https://unsplash.com/photos/fOKx5IOniXk

Kanuckel, A. (2016, April 11). *8 best homemade garden fertilizers.* Farmers' Almanac. https://www.farmersalmanac.com/8-homemade-garden-fertilizers-24258

Kemper, Jonathan (2021). *Person holding green plastic shovel* [Online Photo]. Unsplash. https://unsplash.com/photos/VTXw4_5SsNA

Kitchen Conservatory. (2018, July 19). *How to pick fresh herbs.* YouTube. https://www.youtube.com/watch?v=YpJ-ADj8lts

Knerl, L. (2021, July 24). *The true cost of growing a*

garden. Investopedia. https://www.investopedia.com/financial-edge/0312/the-true-cost-of-growing-a-garden.aspx

Kurtz, L. (2019). *How to grow dandelions*. WikiHow. https://www.wikihow.com/Grow-Dandelions#:~:text=Dandelions%20need%20a%20lot%20of

L.C. Editors. (2018, June 14). *How to infuse water*. Leite's Culinaria. https://leitesculinaria.com/104784/recipes-how-to-make-infused-water.html

Lamp'l, J. (2018). *How to start seeds indoors for gardening*. Joe Gardener. https://joegardener.com/podcast/037-starting-seeds-indoors-pt-1/

Lampeter Permaculture Group. (n.d.). *The history of permaculture*. Lampeter Permaculture Group. Retrieved January 9, 2022, from http://www.lampeterpermaculture.org/what-is-permaculture/the-history-of-permaculture/

Lanzarini, Joshua (2018). *Seeds of Change* [Online Photo]. Unsplash. https://unsplash.com/photos/Vct0oBHNmv4

Leishman, B. (2018). *6 low-maintenance herbs to include in your green wall*. Grow Up. https://blog.growup.green/blogs/growupdates/6-low-maintenance-herbs-to-include-in-your-green-wall

Leron, G. (2017, June 2). *Garlic herb vegan almond cheese spread.* Delightful Adventures. https://delightfuladventures.com/garlic-herb-vegan-almond-cheese-spread/

Link, R. (2017, October 27). *6 science-based health benefits of oregano.* Healthline. https://www.healthline.com/nutrition/6-oregano-benefits

Link, R. (2019). *Stevia safety: Forms, dosage, and side effects.* Healthline. https://www.healthline.com/nutrition/is-stevia-safe

Link, R., & Hill, A. (2018). *13 potential health benefits of dandelion.* Healthline. https://www.healthline.com/nutrition/dandelion-benefits

Lopez-Alt, J. Kenji. (2019). *The best way to store fresh herbs.* Serious Eats. https://www.seriouseats.com/the-best-way-to-store-fresh-herbs-parsley-cilantro-dill-basil#:~:text=Store%20hardy%20herbs%20by%20arranging

Lori. (2019a, January 14). *Vegan seitan bourguignon with rosemary cauliflower mash.* My Quiet Kitchen. https://myquietkitchen.com/vegan-seitan-bourguignon/#recipe

Lori. (2019b, February 28). *Jackfruit salad with mango and dill.* My Quiet Kitchen. https://myquietkitchen.com/jackfruit-mango-and-dill-salad/#recipe

Lori. (2019c, March 11). *Parsley-dill pesto.* My Quiet Kitchen. https://myquietkitchen.com/parsley-dill-pesto/#recipe

Lori. (2020a, February 21). *Oil-free zhoug sauce.* My Quiet Kitchen. https://myquietkitchen.com/oil-free-zhoug-sauce/#recipe

Lori. (2020b, May 22). *Mango-mint yogurt smoothie.* My Quiet Kitchen. https://myquietkitchen.com/mango-mint-yogurt-smoothie/#recipe

Lori. (2020c, December 3). *Vegan rosemary tahini cookies.* My Quiet Kitchen. https://myquietkitchen.com/vegan-rosemary-tahini-cookies/#recipe

Maier, C. (2012). *Which direction to face a vegetable garden.* SFGate. https://homeguides.sfgate.com/direction-face-vegetable-garden-47320.html

Marcott, A. (2017, August 7). *Harvesting herbs 101.* Burpee Home Gardens. https://www.burpeehomegardens.com/blog/2017/08/07/harvesting-herbs-101.html?printerfriendly=true

MasterClass Staff. (2020, November 8). *How to start a backyard garden: 11 steps for new gardeners.* MasterClass. https://www.masterclass.com/articles/how-to-start-a-backyard-garden

McCulloch, M. (2018). *Basil: Nutrition, health benefits, uses and more.* Healthline.

https://www.healthline.com/nutrition/basil

McLeod, J. (2014, April 7). *Medicinal mint: A refreshing remedy*. Farmers' Almanac. https://www.farmersalmanac.com/medicinal-mint-a-refreshing-remedy-18401#:~:text=Place%20the%20mint%20in%20a

Meeks, S. (2014, December 1). *5 possible uses for the bay leaf*. Healthline. https://www.healthline.com/health/5-possible-uses-for-bay-leaf

Michaels, K. (2019). *10 container garden tips for beginners*. The Spruce. https://www.thespruce.com/ten-container-garden-tips-for-beginners-847854

Mount Sinai Health System. (n.d.). *Stinging nettle Information*. Mount Sinai Health System. Retrieved January 21, 2022, from https://www.mountsinai.org/health-library/herb/stinging-nettle#:~:text=Stinging%20nettle%20has%20been%20used

Murano, L. A. (n.d.). *7 ways to use basil as medicine!* Feathers in the Woods. Retrieved January 20, 2022, from https://www.feathersinthewoods.com/2015/07/7-ways-to-use-basil-as-medicine.html#:~:text=Add%202%20tablespoons%20of%20fresh

Najera, Flor (2021). *Hands holding soil* [Online Photo]. Unsplash. https://unsplash.com/photos/Zixns97LP44

Nast, C. (2014, October 15). *Herb powder.* Bon Appétit. https://www.bonappetit.com/recipe/herb-powder

National Health Portal India. (2017). *Introduction and importance of medicinal plants and herbs.* Nhp.gov.in. https://www.nhp.gov.in/introduction-and-importance-of-medicinal-plants-and-herbs_mtl

Netmeds. (2020). *Dill leaves: Astonishing benefits of adding this nutritious herb to your diet.* Netmeds. https://www.netmeds.com/health-library/post/dill-leaves-astonishing-benefits-of-adding-this-nutritious-herb-to-your-diet

Neverman, L. (2017, June 10). *How to infuse herbs in oil, water, vinegar, alcohol or honey.* Common Sense Home. https://commonsensehome.com/how-to-infuse-herbs/

Old Farmer's Almanac. (2021). *Sowing seeds in the vegetable garden.* Old Farmer's Almanac. https://www.almanac.com/direct-sowing-seeds-vegetable-garden

Panoff, L. (2019). *8 surprising health benefits of coriander.* Healthline. https://www.healthline.com/nutrition/coriander-benefits

Patalsky, K. (2017, June 26). *Santa Cruz beach burritos.* Healthy Happy Life. https://healthyhappylife.com/santa-cruz-beach-veggie-burritos/

Pearson, K. (2017, December 13). *8 health benefits of mint*. Healthline. https://www.healthline.com/nutrition/mint-benefits#TOC_TITLE_HDR_9

Phillips, N., & Phillips, M. (n.d.). *Harvesting with the moon*. Red Moon Herbs. Retrieved January 18, 2022, from https://redmoonherbs.com/pages/harvesting-with-the-moon

Planet Natural. (n.d.-a). *How to grow potted herbs (container gardening)*. Planet Natural. Retrieved January 13, 2022, from https://www.planetnatural.com/herb-gardening-guru/potted-herbs/

Planet Natural. (n.d.-b). *How to harvest and dry herbs*. Planet Natural. Retrieved January 17, 2022, from https://www.planetnatural.com/herb-gardening-guru/harvesting-preserving-herbs/

Poindexter, J. (2018, March 31). *6 simple tips for staking your garden plants perfectly every time*. Morning Chores. https://morningchores.com/staking-plants/

Primeau, Nadine (2018). *Assorted condiment lot* [Online Photo]. Unsplash https://unsplash.com/photos/-bLkT8wGV0I

ProFlowers. (2017, May 1). *How to repot a plant: 7 simple steps with pictures*. ProFlowers Blog. https://www.proflowers.com/blog/how-to-repot-a-plant

Properly Rooted. (2020). *How greenhouses work: tips and tricks*. Properly Rooted. https://properlyrooted.com/how-does-greenhouse-work/

Queensland Government. (2013). *Soil pH : Environment, land and water*. Qld.gov.au. https://www.qld.gov.au/environment/land/management/soil/soil-properties/ph-levels

Raman, R. (2018a). *6 benefits of stinging nettle*. Healthline. https://www.healthline.com/nutrition/stinging-nettle

Raman, R. (2018b, December 14). *12 health benefits and uses of sage*. Healthline.
https://www.healthline.com/nutrition/sage

Raman, R. (2021, January 25). *9 herbs and spices that fight inflammation*. Healthline. https://www.healthline.com/nutrition/anti-inflammatory-herbs

Ramya. (2017, June 22). *8 top medicinal uses of chives for skin, hair & health*. Wildturmeric. https://www.wildturmeric.net/chives-medicinal-uses-health-benefits-side-effects/#:~:text=The%20easiest%20way%20to%20use

Read, A. (2020, May 18). *Gardening can influence and benefit your mental health*. AgriLife Today. https://agrilifetoday.tamu.edu/2020/05/18/gardening-can-influence-and-benefit-your-mental-health/

Reilly, K. (2020). *The only tools you need to start a garden*. EatingWell. https://www.eatingwell.com/article/17068/the-only-tools-you-need-to-start-a-garden/

Rinkesh. (2016, December 25). *What is organic gardening and how to start an organic garden.* Conserve Energy Future. https://www.conserve-energy-future.com/start-an-organic-garden.php

Rosalee. (n.d.). *Parsley herb.* Herbal Remedies Advice. Retrieved January 20, 2022, from https://www.herbalremediesadvice.org/parsley-herb.html

RxList. (n.d.). *Lemongrass: Health benefits, uses, side effects, dosage & interactions.* RxList. https://www.rxlist.com/lemongrass/supplements.htm

SanSone, A. (2020, May 20). *20 perennial herbs for the tastiest edible garden ever.* Country Living. https://www.countryliving.com/gardening/garden-ideas/g24793643/best-perennial-herbs/

Scott, E. (2020, December 11). *These are the most difficult herbs to keep alive - and how to look after them.* Metro. https://metro.co.uk/2020/12/11/hardest-herb-plants-grow-at-home-how-to-keep-alive-13736316/

SF Gate Contributor. (2020). *What is the purpose of repotting a plant?* SF Gate. https://homeguides.sfgate.com/pet-safe-fertilizers-13768630.html

Shannon. (2017, October 13). *Baked farro with tomato*

and herbs. Yup, It's Vegan. https://yupitsvegan.com/baked-farro-tomato-herbs/#wprm-recipe-container-7814

Shubrook, N. (2021). *Top 5 health benefits of fennel.* BBC Good Food. https://www.bbcgoodfood.com/howto/guide/health-benefits-fennel

Sincerely Media (2020). *Green plants on brown wooden crate* [Online Photo]. Unplash. https://unsplash.com/photos/Agr1YTrzYPI

Slack, M. (2021, April 2). *10 most common herb gardening mistakes – and how to avoid them.* Homes and Gardens. https://www.homesandgardens.com/news/herb-gardening-mistakes

Smith, M. R. (2016, October 20). *Wind: Why it's a problem and how to reduce it's impact.* Vertical Veg. https://verticalveg.org.uk/growing-in-the-wind/

Spice it up - 11 fun facts about herbs and spices. (2019). East China Schools. https://eastchinaschools.org/wp-content/uploads/bsk-pdf-manager/2019/11/Spice-it-up-Fun-Facts.pdf

Spiske, Markus (2018a). *Support yourself – urban gardening – self-supply – self-sufficiency* [Online Photo]. Unsplash. https://unsplash.com/photos/sFydXGrt5OA

Spiske, Markus (2018b). *Urban Gardening – raising tomatoes for self-support* [Online Photo] Unsplash. https://unsplash.com/photos/4PG6wLlVag4

Spiske, Markus (2021). *Fresh & healthy bio garden herbs harvest – self support, self-sufficiency.* Unsplash. https://unsplash.com/photos/Cijj8Joftjc

Stewart, Jordan (2016). *Shallow focus photograph of green plant* [Online Photo]. Unsplash. https://unsplash.com/photos/uawRUmJw3_0

Sullivan, D. (2020, January 6). *8 benefits of chamomile tea.* Medical News Today. https://www.medicalnewstoday.com/articles/320031#who-should-avoid-chamomile-tea

Svedi, R. (2021). *General care for your herb garden.* Gardening Know How. https://www.gardeningknowhow.com/edible/herbs/hgen/general-care-for-your-herb-garden.htm

Sweetser, R. (2021). *Drying your own herbs for tea.* Almanac. https://www.almanac.com/drying-your-own-herbs-tea#:~:text=up%20a%20cup

Taste of Home. (n.d.-a). *Cheddar and chive mashed potatoes.* Taste of Home. Retrieved January 24, 2022, from https://www.tasteofhome.com/recipes/cheddar-and-chive-mashed-potatoes/

Taste of Home. (n.d.-b). *Cilantro lime shrimp.* Taste of Home. Retrieved January 24, 2022, from https://www.tasteofhome.com/recipes/cilantro-lime-shrimp/

Taste of Home. (n.d.-c). *Cinnamon-basil ice cream.* Taste of Home.

https://www.tasteofhome.com/recipes/cinnamon-basil-ice-cream/

Taste of Home. (n.d.-d). *Dilly cheese ball*. Taste of Home. Retrieved January 24, 2022, from https://www.tasteofhome.com/recipes/dilly-cheese-ball/

Taste of Home. (n.d.-e). *Flaky biscuits with herb butter*. Taste of Home. Retrieved January 24, 2022, from https://www.tasteofhome.com/recipes/flaky-biscuits-with-herb-butter/

Taste of Home. (n.d.-f). *Frozen strawberry-basil* margarita. Taste of Home. https://www.tasteofhome.com/recipes/frozen-strawberry-basil-margarita/

Taste of Home. (n.d.-g). *Herbed feta dip*. Taste of Home. Retrieved January 24, 2022, from https://www.tasteofhome.com/recipes/herbed-feta-dip/

Taste of Home. (n.d.-h). *Rosemary focaccia*. Taste of Home. Retrieved January 24, 2022, from https://www.tasteofhome.com/recipes/rosemary-focaccia/

Taste of Home. (n.d.-i). *Spiced grilled chicken with cilantro butter*. Taste of Home. Retrieved January 24, 2022, from https://www.tasteofhome.com/recipes/spiced-grilled-chicken-with-cilantro-butter/

Taste of Home. (n.d.-j). *Syrian green beans with fresh herbs*. Taste of Home. Retrieved January 24, 2022, from https://www.tasteofhome.com/recipes/syrian-green-beans-with-fresh-herbs/

Taste of Home. (2021, September 22). *Peach-basil lemonade slush*. Taste of Home. https://www.tasteofhome.com/recipes/peach-basil-lemonade-slush/

Taste of Home Editors. (2012, July 26). *How to dry herbs*. Taste of Home. https://www.tasteofhome.com/article/how-to-dry-herbs/

The Editors of Encyclopedia Britannica. (2019a). Traditional Chinese medicine - *herbal therapy*. In Encyclopedia *Britannica*. https://www.britannica.com/science/traditional-Chinese-medicine/Herbal-therapy

The Editors of Encyclopedia Britannica. (2019b). Ayurveda: Medical system. *In Encyclopedia Britannica*. https://www.britannica.com/science/Ayurveda

The Happy Gardening Life. (n.d.). *Herbs sunlight chart: 15 most popular herbs and their sunlight requirements*. The Happy Gardening Life. Retrieved January 20, 2022, from https://thehappygardeninglife.com/blogs/organic-gardening/herbs-sunlight-chart

The Herb Exchange. (2019, March 3). *The importance of soil: the foundation of your garden*. The Herb Exchange. https://theherbexchange.com/the-importance-of-soil-the-foundation-of-your-garden/

The Permaculture Research Institute. (n.d.). *What is permaculture?* The Permaculture Research Institute. https://www.permaculturenews.org/what-is-permaculture/

Tkaczyk, F. (n.d.). *Medicinal herb gardening using permaculture techniques.* Alderleaf Wilderness College. https://www.wildernesscollege.com/medicinal-herb-gardening.html

University of Illinois. (n.d.). *Harvesting, drying and storing herbs.* University of Illinois. Retrieved January 17, 2022, from https://web.extension.illinois.edu/herbs/tips.cfm

Urban Cultivator. (2014, July 3). *How to prune herbs for the best and freshest results.* Urban Cultivator. https://www.urbancultivator.net/prune-herbs-gardening-result/

Urban Filip (2021). *Boy in black and white long sleeve watering garden* [Online photo]. Unsplash. https://unsplash.com/photos/ffJ8Qa0VQU0

US EPA. (2014, February 6). *Do's and don'ts of pest control.* US EPA. https://www.epa.gov/safepestcontrol/dos-and-donts-pest-control

Valerie. (2018, December 21). *Greek goddess vegan quinoa aalad.* Very Vegan Val. https://veryveganval.com/2018/12/21/greek-goddess-vegan-quinoa-salad/

Vanheems, B. (2018). *How to make the best potting mix for starting seeds*. GrowVeg. https://www.growveg.com/guides/how-to-make-the-best-potting-mix-for-starting-seeds/

Vanheems, B. (2020). *4 ways to windproof your garden*. GrowVeg. https://www.growveg.co.uk/guides/4-ways-to-windproof-your-garden/

Vinje, E. (2018, May 23). *How to grow herbs*. Planet Natural. https://www.planetnatural.com/herb-gardening/

WebMD. (n.d.-a). *Calendula tea: Are there health benefits?* WebMD. Retrieved January 21, 2022, from https://www.webmd.com/diet/health-benefits-calendula-tea#:~:text=The%20herb

WebMD. (n.d.-b). *Lemongrass: Overview, uses, side effects, precautions, interactions, dosing and reviews*. WebMD. Retrieved January 21, 2022, from https://www.webmd.com/vitamins/ai/ingredientmono-719/lemongrass#:~:text=The%20leaves%20and%20the%20oil

WebMD Editorial Contributors. (2020a). *Health benefits of bay leaves*. WebMD. https://www.webmd.com/diet/health-benefits-bay-leaves#1

WebMD Editorial Contributors. (2020b). *Lemongrass: Are there health benefits?* WebMD. https://www.webmd.com/diet/lemongrass-health-benefits

Wetherbee, K. (2015, December 29). *Overwintering herbs: Protect rosemary, others from cold, soggy soil.* Oregonlive. https://www.oregonlive.com/hg/2015/12/overwintering_herbs.html

Whitney, C. (2017, November 17). *Permaculture and biodynamics: Sustainable systems of living and growing.* The Ecologist. https://theecologist.org/2013/jul/03/permaculture-and-biodynamics-sustainable-systems-living-and-growing

WikiHow. (2021). *How to divide herb plants.* WikiHow. https://www.wikihow.com/Divide-Herb-Plants

Wild Foods and Medicines. (2016, January 7). *Rosemary.* Wild Foods and Medicines. http://wildfoodsandmedicines.com/rosemary/#:~:text=Rosemary%20can%20be%20utilized%20as

Wong, C. (2019). *The benefits of thymus vulgaris.* Verywell Health. https://www.verywellhealth.com/the-benefits-of-thymus-vulgaris-88803

Zamarripa, M. (2019, April 5). *8 impressive health benefits and uses of parsley.* Healthline. https://www.healthline.com/nutrition/parsley-benefits#TOC_TITLE_HDR_7